PRAISE FOR
THE SEVEN LOST SECRETS OF SUCCESS

"Buy this book, apply these secrets, and your prosperity will be assured."

> —Dan McComas, President, Dan McComas Associates, Marketing & Management Consultants

"This breakthrough book, based on the ideas of a forgotten genius, will help smart marketers increase their effectiveness a minimum of fivefold."

> —Bruce David, publisher of *Starting Smart*

"The principles are sound and sensible, and guaranteed to help any businessperson make more money. Since 99.9 percent of businesses don't use them, anyone putting the seven lost secrets to work will gain an unbelievable edge over the competition."

> —Bob Bly, author of fifty-one business books, including *Selling Your Services*

"One of the most revealing works ever—I literally couldn't put it down. There are life and business success lessons in each chapter."

> —Jim Chandler, President, VistaTron

"Barton was the messiah of business who helped America pull out of the Great Depression. Now he can help *all of us* survive the current recession."

> —Scott Hammaker, CEO, Nashville Party Connection

"An excellent guide to better advertising, better promotions, and better marketing. My copywriting abilities and creative strategies have been strengthened and broadened. I'm awed and inspired."

—Tina Nokes, owner of A-Plus Resume Service

"A passionate book on the timeless, inspiring, perceptive, forceful, and sincere ideas of Bruce Barton, a man nobody really knew, a genius lost in history."

—Jim King, CPA, Houston, Texas

"The rediscovery of these proven principles is the foundation upon which to build a prosperous enterprise."

—Mark Weisser, CEO, Gulf Coast Security Systems

The Seven Lost Secrets *of* Success

The Seven Lost Secrets *of* Success

Million Dollar Ideas of BRUCE BARTON, America's Forgotten Genius

JOE VITALE

John Wiley & Sons, Inc.

Published by John Wiley & Sons, Inc., Hoboken, New Jersey.

Published simultaneously in Canada.

Wiley Bicentennial Logo: Richard I. Pacifico.

All excerpts from Bruce Barton's letters, articles, and books are used here with the kind permission of John B. Wingate, Executive Director of the International Center for the Disabled, owners of Barton's literary rights. Other Bruce Barton materials, including sales letters and advertisements, are copyrighted materials reproduced here for educational purposes only under the fair use provisions of U.S. copyright law.

Limit of Liability/Disclaimer of Warranty: While the publisher and author have used their best efforts in preparing this book, they make no representations or warranties with respect to the accuracy or completeness of the contents of this book and specifically disclaim any implied warranties of merchantability or fitness for a particular purpose. No warranty may be created or extended by sales representatives or written sales materials. The advice and strategies contained herein may not be suitable for your situation. You should consult with a professional where appropriate. Neither the publisher nor author shall be liable for any loss of profit or any other commercial damages, including but not limited to special, incidental, consequential, or other damages.

For general information on our other products and services or for technical support, please contact our Customer Care Department within the United States at (800) 762-2974, outside the United States at (317) 572-3993 or fax (317) 572-4002.

Wiley also publishes its books in a variety of electronic formats. Some content that appears in print may not be available in electronic books. For more information about Wiley products, visit our web site at www.wiley.com.

Library of Congress Cataloging-in-Publication Data:
Vitale, Joe, 1953—

    The seven lost secrets of success : million dollar ideas of Bruce Barton,
America's forgotten genius / Joe Vitale.
      p. cm.
    Previously published: Ashland, OH : VistaTron, c1992. 1st ed. With some revisions.
    Includes bibliographical references.
    ISBN 978-0-470-10810-9 (cloth)
    1. Advertising—Psychological aspects. 2. Success in business. 3. Consumer satisfaction. 4. Social responsibility of business. 5. Barton, Bruce, 1886–1967.
    I. Title. II. Title: Million dollar ideas of Bruce Barton, America's forgotten genius.
HF5822.V58   2007
659.1—dc22   2007012417

Printed in the United States of America.
10 9 8 7 6 5 4 3 2 1

To the late Marian . . .
The loving sunshine who
supported me every step of the way,
no matter what the project was,
or the outcome of it

"One never knows, when he enters an elevator or tears open an envelope or picks up the telephone, what new trick of fortune may be about to be played. Every day is a new series of adventures; around the next corner may lie the event that will change a whole career."

—Bruce Barton, 1928

Contents

About Bruce Barton

"The man has genius."

—*New York Herald Tribune*, 1927

"The Prophet of Advertising."

—*Advertising Digest*, 1949

"Million Dollar Ad Man."

—*Chicago Daily News*, 1944

"The modern philosopher for millions."

—*Tribune Newshawks*, 1945

"He should be advertising's Man of the Century."

—*Printer's Ink*, 1961

"Bruce Barton breathed inspiration."

—*Advertising News*, 1924

Foreword

What a wonderful book! I am delighted that my friend Dr. Joe Vitale has written about a great man who profoundly influenced my life. When I met Bruce Barton, I needed his help badly. I had begun my small advertising business on foot, pushing my two babies before me on a rickety baby stroller with pillows tied on with rope.

There were few sidewalks in the chicken-ranching community of Baldwin Park, California. When the stroller wheel kept coming off, I hit it back on with the heel of my shoe, then picked up the cardboard I had stuffed inside the shoe to cover the holes, shook it out, and stuck it back in. My husband needed my help. I was determined that we would not lose our home in the recession.

During high school, my English teacher had pulled me out of regular English and insisted I take journalism. How I loved it. I was working after school and on weekends in the bakery of a midnight market. After I scrubbed the floors and washed the cases, I wrote articles and poems for *The Moor*, our high school newspaper. So, when my husband and I needed money so badly, I thought of the newspaper.

There were certainly no jobs in that recession period. I persuaded the *Baldwin Park Bulletin* to sell me advertising space at half price. Then I called on the merchants and sold them the space at full price, adding my copy to their products as a shoppers' column I called "Window Wishing." The difference was my profit.

"I write from the customer's viewpoint," I told them enthusiastically. I had no college education. I felt so unprepared in that man's world. But I did have one wonderful thing to help me with my fledging business: the Baldwin Park Library. Every evening I would run over and pick up books on advertising, business, and sales.

It was there I met Bruce Barton. I read all his books, and read them again. I heard his voice in my mind— uplifting, teaching, showing me how.

Then one day the publisher of the *Baldwin Park Bulletin* handed me a notice from the Advertising Association. There was to be a meeting in San Francisco. Bruce Barton would be the speaker!

It took a lot of thinking and planning to put the money together and to arrange for babysitters in order to go. But I made it. I stuffed apples and a package of crackers in my briefcase, because I did not have money for meals. I didn't stay overnight. I just came to hear Mr. Barton.

He had white hair and a slight build, and told stories that enchanted the audience. He said he based his advertising business on two things:

First was a Bible verse: "Agree with your adversary early." He explained that customers relax when you see their side of the situation. When you really understand what your customers want, then it is so easy to show them that your product or service is just what they need to get it. "Your job is to be the buyer's assistant," Mr. Barton said.

Second, he asked the audience if we remembered the third verse of "Mary Had a Little Lamb." Everyone knew the first verse, a few knew the second, but no one could say the third. He recited it as the second great principle of his advertising business:

"Why does the lamb love Mary so?"
The eager children cry.
"Because Mary loves the lamb, you know,"
The teacher did reply.

I remember that I jumped when he hit the lectern with a loud bang as he said that third line. Then he said, "It is about time we quit trying to shear these sheep—and start loving them a little bit!"

I saw immediately that Mr. Barton meant that we must see things through customers' eyes in order to care for their interests and to help them. Because of his teaching, my small advertising business spread into all of Southern California, hiring and training 285 employees who sold over 4,000 continuous-contract advertising accounts. We had four offices. My customers brought me other customers. Mr. Barton's principles were the foundation of my business then, and they still are.

But on that day in San Francisco when I was so young, uneducated, and yearning for knowledge and help for my tiny start-up business, I waited until his speech was over. It took a long time for everyone to shake his hand and finally leave. Then I walked up to Mr. Barton, thinking, "How can I tell him that he is my teacher?"

I only had a moment with him. I reached out my hand to him. He took it in both of his. I looked into his kind eyes and said, "I am the one who *HEARD* you."

Bruce Barton replied, "You are the one I came for."

—Dottie Walters

The late Dottie Walters was the author of several books, including *Speak* and *Grow Rich* and *Never Underestimate the Selling Power of a Woman*. She was also president of Walters International Speakers Bureau and chairman of the board for the American Association of Professional Consultants.

Acknowledgments

Several people helped me create this book.

Thanks to Mrs. Dorothy Caples, widow of the late copywriting king John Caples, for sharing a moment by phone that made my eyes well up with tears. She knew Bruce Barton through her husband's work and gave me a couple of excellent leads for background material. I will not forget talking to her.

Thanks to Greg Manning, Jim King, and Scott Hammaker, three rare friends. Their encouragement and stimulating ideas have always managed to somehow keep my projects alive and keep me moving forward.

Thanks to Dan Starr for his initial research and Bruce Barton bibliography.

Thanks to the Houston Public Library for answering my questions and hunting down copies of old books through their miraculous interlibrary loan system.

Thanks to Colleen of Colleen's Books for her amazing ability to locate out-of-print books on a wide variety of topics. She's been a reliable resource for nearly 20 years.

Thanks to Harold Miller and Christine Schelshorn of the State Historical Society of Wisconsin for their aid in locating specific Bruce Barton materials.

Thanks to John B. Wingate of the International Center for the Disabled for granting permission for me to use excerpts from Bruce Barton's writings in this book.

Several people read earlier versions of this book, or just encouraged me to keep writing, and gave helpful feedback or advice: Murray Raphel, Herschell Gordon Lewis, Debbie Zimmerman, Jerry Twentier, Tina Nokes, Stuart Nokes, Claudette Manning, Carol Marashi, Bob Bly, Dan McComas, Milton Ward, Douglas Norment, Judith Barton Denis, Cliff Leonard, Mark Weisser, Jim Chandler, Martin Parris, Tillie Wier, Lyle Steele, Marquita Anderson, and Deborah Healon all deserve a round of applause.

Jean at the River Oaks Bookstore helped me brainstorm a worthy title for this book.

And thanks, of course, for the late Dottie Walters' friendship, support, and ideas, and for her touching Foreword.

This book has obviously been a team effort.

—Dr. Joe Vitale

www.mrfire.com

"In every human being, whether emperor or cowboy, prince or pauper, philosopher or slave, there is a mysterious something which he neither understands nor controls. It may lie dormant for so long as to be almost forgotten; it may be so repressed that the man supposes it is dead. But one night he is alone in the desert under the starry sky; one day he stands with bowed head and damp eyes beside an open grave; or there comes an hour when he clings with desperate instinct to the wet rail of a storm-tossed boat, and suddenly out of the forgotten depths of his being this mysterious something leaps forth. It over-reaches habit; it pushes aside reason, and with a voice that will not be denied it cries out its questionings and its prayer."

—Bruce Barton, *What Can a Man Believe?*, 1927

Author's Unusual
Introduction

The first edition of this book—published in 1992—started a wild underground movement. One man bought 19,500 copies. Others bought dozens of copies for their staff, their friends, their family, their company. One person left a copy of the book in a hotel room with a note reading, "Read it and leave it for the next person."

I'm in awe. I spent two years researching Bruce Barton, because I wondered what happened to this marketing genius from long ago. He had been a bestselling author and advertising celebrity. His name was once a household word. His ideas made companies rich.

I wanted to know his secrets. After two years of digging through the files, I wrote this book. It went through 19 printings. I updated it, expanded it, and present it now, to you, as a gift of my heart.

Enjoy.

"In 1833 a clerk in the patent office at Washington handed in his resignation.

"There was no more need for a job like his (he wrote). Every possible invention had been conceived and patented: There was nothing left to invent.

"In 1833—and nothing left to invent! Before the railroad had spanned the continent! Before electricity lighted our streets and moved our cars! Before the telephone, or the wireless, or the steam shovel, or the dynamo! At the very threshold of the greatest period of mechanical advance that the world has ever known, this young man threw up his hands. . . .

". . . the world, with all its times of trouble, still moves ahead. No man can play a big part in the world who does not believe in the future of the world."

—Bruce Barton, *It's a Good Old World,* 1920

The Seven Lost Secrets *of* Success

How I Discovered the Lost Secrets

"There is no substitute for love."

—Bruce Barton, 1953

THE ULTIMATE GURU

Business is a great teacher.

It makes you take risks, go for your dreams, face fears, handle your emotions, deal with difficult people, and learn balance. You don't have to do any weird workshops or sign up for any therapy sessions. Go into business and you'll be enrolled in the greatest seminar of all time. And it happens every day, everywhere, to everyone. You can't avoid it.

Though I've done self-help retreats, practiced meditation, walked on fire, and hunted for my inner self, nothing ever compares to the day-by-day challenges of being in business. It's the ultimate guru. It shows you your fears and challenges you to go past them. It shows you your dreams and challenges you to attain them.

Not too many people talk about business in this way.

I thought I was alone in my belief that business could challenge us to be our best, and for a long time I kept silent. But then, while researching advertising methods that were used from the 1920s through 1940s, I found a kindred spirit from an earlier time.

THE MESSIAH OF BUSINESS

Bruce Barton lived from 1886 to 1967—from the post–Civil War period right up to the Vietnam War. Though he had a ringside seat for most of the twentieth century's greatest events, few remember him today. He has somehow fallen through the cracks of history.

When I tried to learn more about Barton, I hit roadblocks. His own advertising firm kept quiet when I asked for information. I couldn't find his relatives, anyone who knew him, or anyone who wanted to tell me anything about him. I began to suspect a cover-up of some sort. For a man who ate with U.S. presidents, made history, and led our country on a quest for prosperity, it seemed odd that he was now forgotten.

I decided to do some investigating.

I couldn't believe what I found.

THE MAN EVERYONE KNOWS

Bruce Barton was so famous in his time that in 1938 an envious fellow wrote, "Almost every day there is a story about a man named Barton. Barton says, Barton suggests, Barton shakes hands, Barton laughs, Barton sneezes. It's Barton, Barton, Barton everywhere."

Barton wrote many books, including a novel, several volumes of inspiring essays, and the 1925 best seller *The Man Nobody Knows*. That book made Barton's name a household word. In it he declared that Jesus was the founder of modern business. The book set an entire nation on a path of service.

When Bobbs-Merrill published the book in 1925, they felt it might sell 500 to 1,000 copies. To everyone's surprise (including the author's), the book shot to fourth place on the best seller list in 1925 and was in first place by 1926. It's still in print today.

Written by a minister's son who was also a prominent businessman, *The Man Nobody Knows* made Barton, at least in the Roaring Twenties, "the man everybody knew."

Barton had contact with every U.S. president and every Republican presidential candidate of the midtwentieth century. He was an enemy of Franklin D. Roosevelt (and FDR openly said so). Barton was also one of the first men in American history to use the media to promote a presidential candidate (Calvin Coolidge). At one point, Barton, a congressman in the 1930s, was named as a potential presidential candidate.

THE SECOND B IN BBDO

As a businessman, Barton helped develop the advertising profession. He was the second "B" in BBDO (the famous Batten, Barton, Durstine, & Osborn agency).

Though Barton was more interested in being a journalist and only wanted to work in advertising part-time, he helped make BBDO the largest ad agency in the world in the 1940s. He created some of the greatest ads in American history, including several to end war (they were never used).

Because of his fame as a writer and businessman, Barton also knew pioneering business leaders, including

Andrew Carnegie and Henry Ford. He was the first to help these giants use advertising to promote their goods.

And as a philanthropist Barton used his skills to help many well-known organizations, such as the American Heart Association, the United Negro College Fund, and the Salvation Army (he coined its slogan "A man is down but he's never out").

Barton's views, revealed in his books, articles, and speeches, shaped our culture. He was a visionary who predicted television before it was invented. He was a revolutionary who supported Jews and blacks and women. He was an optimist who dreamed of prosperity during the Great Depression. He was a national leader who helped middle-class America adjust to a more modern era. He was the original motivational speaker who created inspirational talks that are often referred to even today.

Due to the Depression, World War II, and personal tragedies, Barton's popularity weakened. Today few recall him or his startling message.

BUSINESS CAN SAVE THE WORLD

Barton believed business would save the world. He was a deeply religious man who characterized himself spiritually as a Quaker. But he never felt that heaven would "come all at once." Barton believed that business would help create a heaven on earth.

In 1924 he said that "the millennium, if it is ever coming, is coming through the larger increase and service of business."

On a visit to the White House, Barton told President Calvin Coolidge, "Business is the hope of the world.

Give it a free hand under proper supervision and it will bring in the millennium."

Despite his colorful life, there has never been a study of his groundbreaking ideas.

Until now.

SECRETS TO SUCCESS REVEALED

I believe, like Barton, that responsible actions in business can help us create a world where everyone has a chance for peace, happiness, growth, and prosperity.

This book won't examine Barton's life. Instead, my focus is on Barton's success strategies and on how you can use them today. My belief is that Barton's success at promotion and marketing—his success in all areas of life—was due to these timeless strategies.

Although Barton himself never put his secrets into book form—and his eyes would probably pop open in surprise while reading this book—I'll stand by what I write. I've studied Barton's life, letters, writings, and ads. I've discovered a set of seven secrets that I feel he used, consciously or not, to create his most successful campaigns.

Though one or two of these secrets may be similar to practices used today, you can quickly see that Barton went straight to the heart with his strategies. And he went for a more global impact.

He didn't write an ad to sell a product; he wrote literary vignettes packed with emotion that reveal how a business transforms life as we know it.

More than that, Barton's ideas provide a fresh and lively approach to promotion, publicity, and prosperity, one that goes far beyond any methods that are prevalent today.

The Seven Lost Secrets of Success explains and illustrates each of Barton's secrets. It also includes questions and guidelines so you can use the seven strategies to promote yourself or your own business and attain lasting success and prosperity.

LOST FOR 65 YEARS?

Were Barton's secrets really lost?

Yes.

Today I went to the library to look up three once-famous people: Bruce Barton, Helen Woodward, and Elmer Wheeler. Barton is the subject of this book; Woodward was a pioneer feminist and female copywriter in the 1920s; Wheeler was a nationally known sales trainer and speaker.

Yet I'll bet you never heard of any of them before today. (If it makes you feel better, the library staff hadn't heard of them, either!)

Why not? What happened to these once-great people?

Barton was once a household name. Why doesn't anyone remember him?

Woodward made headlines for her protests and ad copy (she was the first to advertise Mathew Brady's famous Civil War photographs). Why don't we know her name today?

Wheeler wrote best-selling books and created the idea of "selling the sizzle, not the steak." Why is Wheeler forgotten, too?

What happened?

I believe we are so caught up with what's new that we forget about what works. History hasn't forgotten

Barton, Woodward, or Wheeler. We have. Our information age is so overloaded with new ideas, new facts, new reports, new studies, new books, and new news that we can't possibly retain yesterday's news. That's a costly mistake. When we forget the tried-and-true methods, we are forced to relearn them through trial and error (usually a lot of the latter).

Barton had some sensational ideas (so did Woodward and Wheeler, but that's another book). Because we let old knowledge get replaced with new information, we've lost some major secrets to success.

That's why the secrets in this book are "lost secrets."

We've let them become buried.

I simply found them while digging around in old books.

They've benefited me.

Now they can benefit you.

RESULTS GUARANTEED

These lost secrets work. And I can prove it.

I've tested Barton's strategies in my own life. They have given me money, happiness, credibility, a feeling of self-worth, and a sense of contributing to all mankind.

I've seen my clients use these secrets (some knowingly, others by luck), and I've seen them prosper. Their stories, as well as my own, will be shared with you as you turn the pages of this book.

Use these secrets and you will create a legendary, electrifying, prosperous, and unshakable business—a business that just might help bring in the millennium the "messiah of business" had hoped for several decades ago.

> "Many wealthy men have purchased newspapers with the idea of advancing their personal fortunes, or bringing about some political action in which they have a private interest. Such newspapers almost invariably fail. . . . The public has a sixth sense for detecting insincerity; they know instinctively when words ring true."
>
> —Bruce Barton, *The Man Nobody Knows,* 1925

From a 1924 radio broadcast:

"Those of you who were brought up on the Bible will recall the account of Joseph's very remarkable business career. It tells how he left his country under difficulties, and, coming into a strange country, he rose, through his diligence, to become the principal person in the state, second only to the King.

"Now, my friends, the Biblical narrative brings us to that point—the point where Joseph had made a great success and was widely advertised throughout the country; it brings us up to the climax of his career and then it hands us an awful jolt. Without any words of preparation or explanation, it says bluntly:

"'And the King died, and there arose a new King in Egypt which knew not Joseph.'

"Now, that sentence is one of the most staggering lines which has ever been written in a business biography. Here was a man so famous that everybody knew him, and presto, a few people die, a few new ones are born, and nobody knows him. The tide of human life has moved on. . . .

"Now, my friends, let us apply that story to modern business. An hour ago there were in this country sick, in bed, several thousand old folks. It is perhaps indelicate for me to refer to that fact, but it is a fact: In this single hour which has just passed, those old folks have died, and all the goodwill which advertising has built up in their minds has died with them—all the investment made by that past advertising has gone on into another world where the products are not for sale.

"And in this same hour another thing—equally staggering—has happened. There have been born into this country several thousand lusty boys and girls to whom advertised products mean no more than the Einstein theory. They do not know the difference between a Mazda lamp and a stick of Wrigley's chewing gum. Nobody has ever told them that Ivory Soap floats or that children cry for Castoria.

"The tramp of human feet is ceaseless across the state of time. For every day and every hour the King—which is the public—dies; and there arises a new King which knows not Joseph."

—Bruce Barton

WHY YOU MUST ADVERTISE NO MATTER WHAT YOU DO

"You can't advertise today and quit tomorrow. You're not talking to a mass meeting. You're talking to a parade."

—Bruce Barton, 1930

JUST TRY STOPPING

"You are going to have national advertising whether you want it or not!"

—Bruce Barton (year unknown)

The United States Steel Corporation had decided to stop its national advertising. Barton went to Pittsburgh to confront the managers. He told them they could cancel their advertising if they wanted, but that a different kind of advertising would continue.

"It is the advertising given you by politicians with axes to grind—by newspapers that hope to build circulation by distorting your acts—by all other operators in the field of public opinion, some unfriendly and some merely misinformed."

Then Barton hit them with a thunderbolt:

"Can you afford to take the risk of having all your advertising emanate from sources beyond your control?"

U.S. Steel renewed its advertising campaigns.

YOUR TRUE KING

Your customer is king. (And if you are working for a boss, your boss is your customer.)

But your customers and clients do not know what you can do for them unless you tell them.

And you must also *keep* telling them.

Every day a new set of customers appears. A new generation is born. Children become buying adults. Adults switch jobs, develop new interests and lifestyles, and have new needs and desires. If you do not let these people know about you and your services, they will not know to call you. They will go to whomever they have read about, heard about, or seen advertised. These new buyers will be the new king and they will not know of you.

Either advertise and continue to advertise or a new breed of customers will arise who will ignore you for one simple reason: They won't know you exist.

In 1920 Bruce Barton wrote, "You think that you have told your story to the world, and that therefore your task is done. I tell you that overnight a new world has been born that has never heard your story."

You can offer the best service, the lowest prices, and free incentives for every man, woman, and child who walks through your door—but if no one knows of you and your business, no one will come.

"Elias Howe invented the sewing machine, but he could not get women to buy it," Barton said in a 1934 speech. "He lived in poverty, and was reduced to the ignominy of attending his wife's funeral in borrowed clothes. A whole generation of women who might have had their work made easier by his invention lived without its service because there was no advertising to tell them about it."

And consider Mozart. He wrote the world's greatest music, yet died penniless. Those who followed him, who knew how to advertise, grew wealthy by marketing Mozart's works.

You can be the best worker, the smartest in your field, a person who has won awards for your dedication and excellence—but if you don't somehow let people know about your talents, they won't ever call you or ask for your help.

Note this: When the Great Depression rocked the country in the 1930s, most companies stopped all their advertising. It seemed like a logical move. But many of the companies who continued to advertise are still around today!

There's no way around it.

You *must* advertise.

HOW TO ADVERTISE

I get a lot of mail.

It's amazing to see so many people wasting their money on advertising that doesn't work. It makes me gag. The ads, though often creative, don't get results. The flyers all look alike. The sales letters are impotent. Yet people keep dumping their money into this so-called advertising and they keep praying for results.

Eventually they go bankrupt and a new advertiser shows up to offer the same product or service in the same limp way. After a while they fold and someone else comes along. And so it goes—since the process continues, few ever stop to ask if the efforts are actually working.

It's time for a change.

This book will help you promote yourself (or your business) in surprising and effective ways—ways already tested decades ago by a man who used the methods to promote legendary businessmen like Henry Ford and Andrew Carnegie, and even U.S. presidents like Calvin Coolidge and Dwight Eisenhower.

Now it's your turn.

The secrets presented in this book will help you achieve lasting prosperity and success. You'll still have to design ads that get attention and write letters that get results, but you'll have the edge over everyone else. You'll have the forgotten secrets of an advertising legend—a man who was prosperous and successful in all areas of life—on your side.

> "Advertising is the very essence of democracy. An election goes on every minute of the business day across the counters of hundreds of thousands of stores and shops where the customers state their preferences and determine which manufacturer and which product shall be the leader today, and which shall lead tomorrow."
>
> —Bruce Barton, 1955

"Here is an important distinction that many people overlook:

"God made the world; but He does not make your world.

"He provides the raw materials, and out of them every man selects what he wants and builds an individual world for himself.

"The fool looks over the wealth of material provided, and selects a few plates of ham and eggs, a few pairs of trousers, a few dollar bills—and is satisfied.

"The wise man builds his world out of wonderful sunsets, and thrilling experiences, and the song of the stars, and romance and miracles.

"Nothing wonderful ever happens in the life of a fool—an electric light is simply an electric light; a telephone is only a telephone—nothing unusual at all.

"But the wise man never ceases to wonder how a tiny speck of seed, apparently dead and buried, can produce a beautiful yellow flower. He never lifts a telephone receiver or switches on an electric light without a certain feeling of awe."

—Bruce Barton, *More Power to You*, 1917

Secret #1:
Reveal the Business Nobody Knows

"In the long run no individual prospers beyond the measure of his faith."
—Bruce Barton, 1921

A NATION OF STEEL

Bruce Barton dug deep to find out how a business served a global need or contributed to the growth of the country.

When he and Roy Durstine landed the United States Steel Corporation account in 1935, Barton helped whip up an ad that made history. He said Andrew Carnegie "came to a land of wooden towns . . . and left a nation of steel."

This type of strategy changed the perspective of everyone. People were no longer buying a product called steel; they were supporting a mission to improve the lifestyle of a nation.

How does your business serve life? How do you contribute to the improvement of lives?

You have to look past the obvious. You may be running a hamburger stand. But are you just selling burgers? Aren't you doing something more—maybe keeping people alive and healthy so they can enjoy their lives more and be happier?

HOW YOU CAN LIVE FOREVER

I sometimes help people write books. But books aren't my only product. I am in the business of giving immortality.

Let me explain.

A book is a way for you to live forever. When you write a book, you put yourself in that book. And you also create something that will live beyond you. Just look at the man we are talking about: Bruce Barton. He died in 1967. But his writings have touched me (and now you) from beyond the grave.

Barton used this tactic to help him write his most famous book.

The Man Nobody Knows made Jesus vibrant for millions of people. Most people thought (and still think) of Jesus as a mild type of savior. But Barton said Jesus was physically strong from being a carpenter, healthy from walking in the open air every day, popular because He was invited to parties and attracted little kids, and a wise leader because He took 12 unknown men (fishermen!) and made them salespeople for His organization—one that has spanned the globe and touched millions for thousands of years.

In 1920, Barton wrote of Jesus: "He was at a wedding party. The wine had given out. So He performed His first miracle. Just to save a hostess from embarrassment—and He thought it worth a miracle. Just to save a group of simple folk from having their hour of joy cut short—it was for such a cause, He thought, that His divine power had been entrusted to Him."

Nobody ever told *me* that before! I now see Jesus with new eyes because of Barton's explanation. Barton revealed the man I never knew.

THE ADVERTISING NOBODY KNOWS

Barton also used this strategy on his own profession.

When people complained that advertising was misleading or corrupt, he responded by "revealing the business nobody knows."

The late John Caples, author and friend of Barton, once wrote in his diary that Barton "took the profession of advertising and told what wonders it is accomplishing in improving living standards—how it is forwarding the progress of the human race—how it is really a noble profession."

Barton himself said, "If advertising is sometimes longwinded, so is the United States Senate. If advertising has flaws, so has marriage."

Elsewhere Barton said, "As a profession advertising is young; as a force it is as old as the world. The first words uttered, 'Let there be light,' constitute its character. All nature is vibrant with its impulse."

What Barton did was reframe the way people viewed his profession. And it worked. His agency became one of the largest in the world.

THE PRESIDENT NOBODY KNOWS

When Barton was named as a possible candidate for the U.S. presidency in 1932, he wrote an article for *Cosmopolitan* magazine that "revealed the President nobody knows."

Most of us consider the president's job to be high-risk, high-stress, high-profile—a controversial and demanding position. Not Barton. He said two of his first official acts would be to buy a horse and join two golf clubs.

"The President should never be tired or worried. He should be fresh, clear-minded, full of power and decision. Thus, when his two or three big opportunities arise, he will be prepared to speak the word or perform the act that will fire the imagination of the country."

Barton went on to say that our presidents have never been very relaxed. He presented a new president—one nobody had ever imagined before—a president who was human.

Although Barton was not elected president, his unique campaign strategy made him more real—and more memorable and endearing—to thousands of people who never knew him.

WHAT PEOPLE REALLY WANT

The way to perform this first strategy of "revealing the business nobody knows" is to think of what people really want.

Cosmetic companies don't sell lipstick; they sell romance (and sex). They know women want to love and be loved. Lipstick is a device to attain the desired end. To "reveal the business nobody knows," a cosmetics firm would focus on the romance and sex derived from using its product.

People want: security, sex, power, immortality, wealth, happiness, safety, health, recognition, and love.

How do you (or your business) deliver any of those essential needs?

I mentioned a hamburger stand earlier. Instead of focusing solely on hamburgers, what if the owners started selling "health"? They could bill the business as the first hamburger stand that caters to your health. They could say, "Our burgers will give you energy and vitamins," or something to that effect. They could "reveal the business nobody knows."

Most people sell what they have in front of them. In other words, if you're selling a shirt, you show the shirt. But a way to "reveal the shirt nobody knows" is to show how the shirt satisfies a more deep-seated desire. Maybe the shirt is made of special material that allows your skin to breathe, thereby giving you comfort. You have to look beyond the obvious.

Take baking soda. Arm & Hammer has us putting its product on our toothbrushes and in our refrigerators. They are clever people. They keep revealing other uses for baking soda. But Bruce Barton would have gone further and shown how baking soda serves the world. Had Barton handled the Arm & Hammer baking soda account, we'd be crop-dusting the planet with the stuff to clear the air of pollution.

When Bruce Barton was handed the U.S. Steel account, he could have written a relatively good ad that said, "U.S. Steel is the best in the business."

Instead, Barton looked deeper. He wanted to reveal how the steel business served the more basic needs of people. As a result, he came up with the now-famous ad (listed in *The 100 Greatest Advertisements of All Time*): Andrew Carnegie "came to a land of wooden towns . . . and left a nation of steel."

THE WAR NOBODY KNOWS

Barton hated war.

He lived through our country's worst wars—from World War I right up to the Vietnam War. He knew it was a hopeless activity. "Nobody can win," he said.

In 1932 he created a series of advertisements to "reveal the war nobody knows." He wanted to drive home the costs and pains of war. He wanted to awaken people to the tragic reality of war. Barton knew that future wars would involve airplanes, big business, and even chemicals. And he wanted to stop it by advertising "this Hell!" One of his ads read:

SO THE LUSITANIA WENT DOWN

Well, what of it?

"What of it?" you cry. "The whole world was shocked. For days the newspapers talked of nothing else."

Well, but what of it? After all, it was a little thing.

How many Lusitanias would have to go down to carry all the dead and missing soldiers and the dead civilians of the great World War?

One Lusitania a day.

For a year.

For 10 years.

For 25 years.

For 50 years.

One Lusitania a day for 70 years, or one a week, beginning nearly a century before the discovery of America by Columbus and continuing to the present hour.

That is the number of Lusitanias that would be required to carry the dead. The dead of all nations who died in the war.

That ad and four others were used as illustrations in an article by Barton in 1932 (before World War II) in *American* magazine. But they never ran as advertisements. And the country's failure to listen to Bruce Barton's pleas to "reveal the war nobody knows" allowed history to record further horrors. You can see the ads that never ran in the back of this book, beginning on page 173.

THE GASOLINE NOBODY KNOWS

At a 1925 talk to the American Petroleum Institute, Barton told his audience they weren't selling gasoline at all.

> "My friends, it is the juice of the fountain of eternal youth that you are selling. It is health. It is comfort. It is success. And you have sold it as a bad-smelling liquid at so many cents a gallon. You have never lifted it out of the category of a hated expense."

Barton explained his shocking position with a story about Jacob, whose poor immigrant parents had no gasoline and therefore no respite from the dingy neighborhood where they lived under the shadow of ugly smokestacks.

> "Not so with Jacob. He works in the smoke of the city to be sure, but he lives in the suburbs and has his own garden. His children are healthier; they go to better schools. On Sunday he packs up a picnic lunch and bundles the family into the car and has a glorious day in the woods or at the beach. . . .

> "And all this is made possible by a dollar's worth of gasoline!"

THE BUSINESS NOBODY KNOWS

When big-league companies such as Sears or Hallmark Cards sponsor television programs (an idea created by Barton), they reveal themselves to be caring. "Brought to you by Hallmark" lets you know Hallmark is human— while also planting its name in your mind.

Barton began a book in 1928 designed to reveal business as a major force for positive change. Many people fear or flee business because they think it's corrupt. Sometimes business *is* corrupt. But Barton saw business shaping society and helping it grow. Barton's book was going to "reveal the business nobody knows." (Probably due to the crash of 1929, Barton shelved the project.)

In 1957 Barton offered to help DuPont. He said he would create new advertising that "would dramatize the company's research, its dependence on and interrelation with smaller businesses, its success in managing to get along all these years without any strikes, the home life of its employees, and the tremendous contribution to the comfort and health of the American people as a result of what has gone on in the laboratories."

In short, Barton wanted to "reveal the DuPont nobody knows."

TEACH THEM WHY

Revealing your business means educating people about what you do.

Most businesses tell a partial story. They run a series of short ads because they believe no one will read any single long ad. But as the great copywriter Claude Hopkins declared in his famous 1923 book, *Scientific Advertising:* "People are not apt to read successive advertisements on any single line, no more than you read a news item twice, or a story. So present to the reader, when once you get him, every important claim you have."

In 1952 Barton advised the New York Stock Exchange to "find some way to translate their story into terms of human life and the reader's self-interest." He also suggested that the stock exchange reveal its business by pointing out that it had 600 listed firms and 1,300 members in 73 cities and that it was a money-saving institution.

Barton was encouraging his clients to tell their whole story. He knew people would be understanding if you explained your business. "Reveal the business nobody knows" by telling people what you are all about. You still have to be brief, clear, and interesting, of course. But if you tell your story, you will win more loyal customers than if you don't.

Look at it this way:

If I tell you I charge $2,500 an hour for my services, you might wince.

But if I explain that I require that fee because of my education, experience, and expenses; because of the personalized, rare service I deliver; and because of how much money I can help make for you, then you would feel better about my fee.

Why? Since you now have an explanation of why I charge what I do, you are more likely to accept the fee.

People are logical *and* emotional. You have to appeal to both sides to capture their loyalty.

THE YOU NOBODY KNOWS

Your business does more than provide a service.

Once you "reveal the business nobody knows"—to yourself and to your clients—you discover how business transforms life itself.

Another Barton example (from 1925):

"The General Electric Company and the Western Electric Company find the people in darkness and leave them in light; the American Radiator finds them cold and leaves them warm; International Harvester finds them bending over their sickles the way their grandfathers did and leaves them riding triumphantly over their fields."

And here's Barton describing how the automobile made us lords over the earth:

"The automobile companies find a man shackled to his front porch and with no horizon beyond his own dooryard and they broaden his horizon and make him in travel the equal of a King."

—Bruce Barton, 1925

Bruce Barton: "Here is a man who knew Lincoln, who shook his hand, and heard his voice, and watched him laugh at one of his own funny stories. Did you feel, as you talked to him, 'I am in the presence of a personality so extraordinary that it will fascinate men for centuries'?"

Russell Conwell: "Not at all. He seemed a very simple man, I might almost say ordinary, throwing his long leg over the arm of his chair and using such commonplace, homey language. . . . So it was hard to be awed in the presence of Lincoln; he seemed so approachable, so human and simple."

—Conversation between Bruce Barton (age 34) and Russell Conwell (age 78), author of *Acres of Diamonds*, 1921

SECRET #2:
USE A GOD
TO LEAD THEM

"In each generation are a few men who catch a vision so big and steadfast that in the pursuit of it they lose all thought of their own interest or advantage."

—Bruce Barton, 1918

RIDING TO HER DEATH

"Tonight will make history. This will be the turning point in the campaign. The General must be expertly stage-managed, and when he speaks, it must be with the understanding and the mercy and the faith of God."

1952. Bruce Barton was secretly guiding Dwight David Eisenhower into a position of power. Barton was using the same strategy he used for Calvin Coolidge and for Herbert Hoover: Barton was creating "a god to lead them."

The son of a famous minister, Barton was always drawing inspiration from religion. It's no accident that his most famous book was about Christ (and his second most famous book was about the Bible).

Barton used emotionally packed archetypes in his ads. One of his most famous ads, done quickly and almost by accident, included a sketch of Marie Antoinette "riding to her death." He asked, "Have you ever read her tragic story?"

By drawing a connection to an emotionally charged mother-child figure from history, Barton was able to touch the deepest emotions of people. (And that ad for Dr. Charles William Eliot's "five-foot shelf" of Harvard Classics pulled eight times better than all previous ads for the same set of books.)

THE SERVICE GURU

When Ron McCann hired me to write his book on service, he intuitively began to use this secret. During the process of creating *The Joy of Service*, Ron one day announced that he was a "a guru for service."

Was this his ego talking? Maybe. None of us are here without an ego. But Ron was letting people know that he was the spokesperson for service. By calling himself the "service guru" he created a type of god for people to follow.

People love experts. Authorities are more easily listened to because we assume they know what they're talking about. It always amazes me that anyone who writes a book becomes an expert on the subject of that book—even if the book is crammed with erroneous information.

Become an authorized expert in your field and you are seen as a type of god. Like Ron McCann, you establish yourself as *the* person to talk to, listen to, and hire. Ron's business skyrocketed once his book came out. It was translated into Spanish in 1991. As the "service guru," Ron now travels back and forth between the United States and Mexico giving talks on service.

BECOME THE EXPERT

Companies are always using celebrities in their ads, because celebrities are types of gods to us. We know them, love them, and respect them. If you think your favorite film star uses a certain product, you are more inclined to buy that product. You'll follow your god right into the store.

It's more powerful to do what Ron McCann did. Set *yourself* up as the expert in your field. Writing a book (or hiring someone to do it) will work. It positions you as an expert.

- Tom Peters became the expert on excellence when his book came out.
- Lee Iaccoca's autobiography and book on leadership became best sellers.
- Harvey Mackay's speaking career soared when his books hit the stands.
- The late Dave Thomas, founder of Wendy's, wrote a book on his ideas for achieving success.
- Dan Kennedy writes books to draw in new customers.
- Donald Trump and Richard Branson have each written several books.
- And my book on P.T. Barnum, *There's a Customer Born Every Minute*, makes the public aware of him.

And the businesses of every one of these people improved. (Had you ever heard of Harvey Mackay before he wrote a book?)

If you feel you aren't smart enough or important enough to be considered an expert on anything, think about what Bruce Barton wrote in 1920:

> "Lincoln said a wonderfully wise thing one day. 'I have talked with great men,' he said, 'and I cannot see wherein they differ from others.'"

By the way, Barton's father was an expert on the life of Abraham Lincoln. He wrote several biographies of

Lincoln and was regarded as an authority in his field of expertise. You probably have skills you aren't even aware of. When I meet with clients I sit and listen to their stories. Buried within their monologues usually are golden book ideas. I point them out and then help them create a book.

The end result is a product they can sell (the book) and a ticket to instant credibility. In addition to all that, a book is a traveling PR agent, selling you and your message even when you aren't present.

DOUG JOHNSON'S SECRET

One summer many years ago I was invited on the Doug Johnson radio show. Doug is one of the most popular media people in all of Texas. His talk show is a major hit in Houston. It was exciting to be asked on his show. And though the show was fun, what Doug and I talked about off the air was even more exciting and revealing.

Doug told me he had written a novel. Since my expertise is in nonfiction, I suggested he try his hand at writing a how-to book.

"I wouldn't know what to write about," Doug said.

Now, here's a talk show host with decades of experience under his belt in handling all types of people, and yet he didn't see the diamond in his own backyard.

"Doug, you are an expert in dealing with people and getting them to open up," I said. "You've seen people scared stiff and yet you helped them relax. You've seen people who talked too much and yet you managed to slow them down. And you do it all with such gentleness and charm!"

"So?"

"So write a book on how to have conversations with people. Or write a book on how to talk in any situation. Or write a book on how to make people relax and open up under any circumstances. Most people don't know what you know, Doug!"

Then this wonderful man started to tell me some stories about people he had seen over the years.

"One woman was a sex therapist who wanted to know if she could say anything on the air," Doug recalled. "Just as we went live she asked, 'Is it okay to say !@X%$!!?' My face turned beet red!"

I laughed and said, "Doug, those are the stories people would love to read about. You could use them to illustrate your points."

Doug Johnson's eyes lit up.

He heard me. *He* was a famous talk show host, a celebrity in Texas, yet it had never occurred to him that he knew anything!

His expertise was a secret he kept from himself.

HOW TO CREATE A MIRACLE

When Ron McCann's book was off the press and he and I were sitting in his office, resting after the long effort to create it, I said, "Ron, do you realize we've created a miracle?"

He asked what I meant.

"This book is going to go out into the world and be read by people you don't know, and touch people you'll never meet, and start conversations that you'll never hear," I explained. "Our book is like another life form. It will move and change lives all by itself. People will talk about it, and talk about you, and you may never know it. That's a miracle."

Bruce Barton wrote several books (all but one now out of print). They established him as an authority. At one point the offices of BBDO in New York were packed with people wanting the legendary Bruce Barton to create their ads.

Why? Because Barton was seen as a type of god. He was extremely successful, and everyone wanted to see if some of his success would rub off on them.

It's clear to me that BBDO became a famous advertising agency largely due to the fame of Bruce Barton himself. Frank Rowsome Jr., in his delightful book, *They Laughed When I Sat Down*, said Barton was BBDO's "resident deity."

Barton was a best-selling author, a community leader, a philanthropist, a politician, and a respected authority in business. He was, in effect, a type of "god" people wanted to follow.

And Barton still lives—through the miracles of his books.

Back in 1920 Bruce Barton wrote this thought-provoking statement:

> "If you have anything really valuable to contribute to the world, it will come through the expression of your own personality—that single spark of divinity that sets you off and makes you different from every other living creature."

How can *you* establish yourself as a type of god?

POST AND CROCKER AND EARHART

Here are three quick examples of goddesses for you to think about.

While working on the American Tobacco Company account, Barton suggested getting Emily Post (a clear goddess) to do an advertisement on the etiquette of smoking. ("Don't smoke in elevators. Don't light a cigarette until after the salad.")

Did you know that "Betty Crocker" is a fictional character? Barton co-created her in order to attract customers to buy General Mills products. Clearly Betty Crocker is a goddess well loved by the masses.

Finally, the American Tobacco Company got Amelia Earhart to promote Lucky Strike cigarettes in 1928 (even though Earhart did not smoke). While this last example violates another Barton secret (sincerity), you can easily see that spokespeople are often perceived as gods or goddesses by the masses.

"Every man in a big position knows in his own heart that forces entirely outside himself have played a large part in his making."

—Bruce Barton, 1928

"Many of us are afraid this expenditure of compassion will drain away our energy, deplete us for our own tasks. But the dynamics of compassion defy the ordinary laws of energy. We discover that, like Antaeus in the ancient myth, our strength is doubled by compassionate contact with the blessed earth of humanity. . . .

"Compassion belongs to the other great band of noble virtues—tolerance, sympathy, understanding—all marching under the banner of love."

—Bruce Barton, 1942

Secret #3:
Speak in Parables

"Money has a perverse habit of evading those who chase it too hard, and of snuggling up to folks who are partially unmindful to it."

—Bruce Barton, 1928

SNAP, CRACKLE, POP

Bruce Barton was one of the few people in history able to write ads, essays, articles, and full-length books—all with equal impact.

Part of his secret was due to his ability to write simple, snappy copy that was also rich in depth and meaning. He did this by creating stories that reached the common worker as well as the intellectual. It's also a technique that Barton's two models, Jesus Christ and Abraham Lincoln, used to create unforgettable and highly persuasive "ads."

In 1951, Barton wrote in a private memo,

"[Jesus] told His listeners stories [such as] the story, 'A certain man went down from Jerusalem to Jericho and fell among thieves.' Every one of his listeners knew some man who had fallen among thieves on that dangerous Jerusalem turnpike. They listened to the story and remembered it. If He had said, 'I want to talk to you about why you should be a good neighbor,' nobody would have listened."

HYPNOTIC STORIES

Stories move people. As author Jean Houston once told me, "We are storied people. We group the experiences of our lives into stories. We gossip in story format. We don't see life as a river; we see it as a story with a definite beginning, middle, and end. Stories make life easier to understand."

Practitioners of neurolinguistic programming (NLP) have discovered that stories are a powerful way to persuade people. Milton Erickson, the legendary hypnotist, was known for his therapeutic stories. Stories are a way for a message to be delivered indirectly.

As I explained in my book, *Hypnotic Writing*, a story with your sales message seeps in under the listener's or reader's awareness. If you tell someone to do something in a direct, forceful manner, they'll probably resist. But if you give the same order as a suggestion within the frame of story, they'll probably do exactly what you want.

Let me explain.

HOW TO SELL BAD PRODUCTS

John Caples was a brilliant copywriter who worked with Bruce Barton. Maxwell Sackheim was another famous copywriter who probably knew Barton. Both of these legends had experiences that illustrate the power of "story selling."

Both of these advertising giants were assigned the task of writing ad copy for books that were actually bad. How do you sell a product that isn't any good? How would you do it?

Both Caples and Sackheim, working independently of each other, wrote letters that are still talked about today,

decades after they were written. The letters were so mes-
merizing that they *still* cause those bad books to sell.

How did they do it?

They wrote their ads as stories. They talked about
how they were changed by reading the book they
wanted to sell. Without going into any ethical questions
here, pause and consider how powerful their stories
must have been.

If I told you, "These shoes will make your feet feel
better," you'd shrug your shoulders and move on.

But if I told you about how my feet once ached so
painfully that I cried in bed at night, and how I one day
discovered a pair of amazing shoes that made my feet
feel like they were on air cushions, you'd perk up and
listen.

Why? Because I told you a story.

STORY SELLING

A parable is a story. Barton wrote stories laced with subtle meaning. Caples and Sackheim wrote stories that
made their sales letters irresistible. Every great speaker
(and Barton was an electrifying speaker) knows that a
good story can deliver the point better than anything
else imaginable.

What are the success stories in your business?

Who bought your product or service and was transformed? Where have you worked and made a difference? Those are your parables, the stories that sell
people on what you offer.

When I was selling a software product, a customer called and said, "Joe, I was skeptical when I saw your letter about the program. But I took a chance. Boy, was I surprised! I turned on my computer, the program began to talk to me, and when I was all done I had written a letter that brought me over one thousand dollars! I have the check in my hands right now."

That's a persuasive story. It's a story that also sells other people on buying the program.

When I tell people that I write books, they nod politely while thinking of what they need at the store. But when I tell a story about helping a young speaker create a book and now the speaker is traveling worldwide and getting rich, people listen.

HE DIED A MILLIONAIRE

When I was working up an ad to sell the first edition of this book, I decided to use a "story selling" technique.

I could have written some clever ad saying this book would make you rich and famous and help you make money while you sleep.

I *could* have done that. But I didn't.

I decided to tell you a story . . . about a man who was once so famous his name was a household word . . . about a man who wrote a best-selling book that inspired a nation to deliver service . . . about a man who helped create one of the largest advertising firms in the world . . . about a man who ate with presidents and kings and served in Congress . . . about a man who lost a wife, a daughter, a son . . . and died an unknown millionaire in 1967.

In short, I decided to sell you with the power of a story.

And since you are now reading this book, apparently the story-selling approach worked.

A BARTON STORY SELLS ME

One of Bruce Barton's books was the 1927 volume *What Can a Man Believe?* In it Barton tells a story that sold me on an idea—nearly 70 years after Barton told the story!

"Some years ago a crumpled and dejected citizen came to my office," Barton begins. The man was a sales manager with a reputation for writing effective sales letters. But suddenly this man was out of work and depressed—even suicidal. Barton led the man to a window.

"Look out there at those buildings," Barton said. "All filled with offices. Business offices. Offices of people who have goods to sell and most of whom don't know how to sell them."

Then Barton challenged the man (another Barton tactic).

"You say you can write sales letters. This is your great chance to prove it. Write those people a letter that will sell them the idea that they need you to help them sell their goods."

The man accepted the challenge. He was soon earning more than $25,000 a year—in the early 1920s!

That's a powerful story. When I read it, something awakened in me. I realized I could do what Barton advised that man to do. Somehow Barton's message—and his challenge—reached across seven decades and out of the pages of an old book to touch me.

And months later, when a young copywriter came to me complaining that he couldn't get work, I led him to an open window, pointed at all the buildings outside, and told him the story I just told you.

It's the power of a parable. And it works.

A MIRACLE LETTER

This Barton strategy helped me create one of the most celebrated letters of my career.

In 1991 I met a man who deeply influenced my life. Jonathan Jacobs was a Houston therapist with a spiritual philosophy I respect. After only two sessions with him I sat down and wrote a sales letter for him. Note how this letter is sincere (another Barton secret) and how it tells a compelling story:

Dear Friend,

Jonathan Jacobs has blown my head off twice now. He's a Zen master, psychic bear, and psychological samurai—all wrapped into a wonderfully warm and gentle fellow. Sound too hard to believe? Then get a load of this:

I've hung out with gurus, done more workshops than I care to remember, read books, written books, walked on hot coals, asked "Who am I?" for hours on end, listened to tapes, and led meditation groups, encounter groups, self-help groups, and more.

I've been "on the path" for over 10 years now. But nothing—*nothing!*—has had the sweeping and dramatic effect on my life as my sessions with Jonathan.

My first experience with Jonathan's BodyMemory work was electrifying. Under this man's wise guidance I relived past experiences and healed old hurts. Some of those old hurts were buried and damn uncomfortable to recall. But I let them come and I let them go. And somehow, by letting them go, there was a ripple effect that *changed everything* in my life.

Within a few days my prosperity increased. Did I say increased? My income actually and unexpectedly *doubled*. Though it happened like magic, I credit Jonathan's help in changing limiting beliefs to expanded ones for the miracle.

And speaking of miracles, I also transformed my relationship with my father. On Jonathan's table I "breathed through" some old scenarios with my dad. Off Jonathan's table I felt better about Pop. I actually missed him. My father's home is a thousand miles away, and amazingly an out-of-state client of mine suddenly hired me for a consultation—in his state, which just happened to be an hour's drive from my father's house. This client also agreed to drive me to my dad's home so I could drop in for a surprise visit!

Jonathan's work doesn't make logical sense, however. That's why the man consistently blows my mind to smithereens and I end up, after each session, walking around "with no head." I'm sure there is a logic to Jonathan's work, but it's based on divine wisdom, not Joe's wisdom. Don't ask me to explain it.

I encourage you to call Jonathan. Tell him I sent you. Sample his medicine. And get ready for some amazing and truly wonderful changes.

Sincerely,

Dr. Joe Vitale

MARSHALL FIELD

During the Roaring Twenties, Barton had numerous famous accounts. One of them was Marshall Field & Company. Most of the advertising Barton created for this popular department store was based on the parable technique. For example:

> "Once upon a time an obscure actor who was playing in Chicago came to Marshall Field & Company to have a pair of shoes repaired. Years later, at the height of his fame, he talked to our girls on the tenth floor. . . ."

Another example:

> "There is a man in this store who clearly remembers selling apparel to Mrs. Abraham Lincoln in 1874. . . ."

Do you *feel* how those examples begin like stories?

Stories give color and life to your message. They involve people, entertain them, and stick with them.

What are *your* parables?

NAPOLEON INSPIRES BARTON

On the last leg of my quest to learn everything I could about Bruce Barton, I flew up to Madison, Wisconsin, home of over 150 boxes stuffed with letters, articles, and manuscripts by and about Barton. What I noticed about Barton's writings was this: Nearly every one of those 2,000 articles and essays was in a story format. Pick up any article, look at the first line, and suddenly you're drawn into a story.

Barton knew stories were the best teachers—and sales-people. Stories hold attention, enrich our lives, and—if they're well done—inspire and motivate us.

In one 1919 article Barton talked about Napoleon Bonaparte. The whole message of the piece was "Feel confident and go get a job." But Barton never said that. Instead, he told a story about how his reading about the life of Napoleon (a favorite Barton hero) gave him the courage and confidence to go out and *demand* a new job.

Barton absorbed the spirit of the great emperor and then hit the streets in search of work. As good stories go, this one ended happily. Barton got the job he wanted—within a week.

And we readers get the message—all from his delightful story.

> "I have been out of a job three times in my life. Each time I made a survey of my surroundings and discovered that there was work to be done, though not the same kind of work I had been doing."
>
> —Bruce Barton, 1941

> "By a change of thought the yeoman of England became the unconquerable army of Cromwell. By a change of thought a handful of fishermen of Palestine transformed human history."
>
> —Bruce Barton, 1920

> "I hope I may never be guilty of writing anything intended to make poor people contented with their lot.
>
> "I would rather be known as one who sought to inspire his readers with a divine discontent.

"To make men and women discontented with bad health, and to show them how, by hard work, they can have better health.

"To make them discontented with their intelligence, and to stimulate them to continued study.

"To urge them on to better jobs, better homes, more money in the bank.

"But it does not harm, in our striving after these worthwhile things, to pause once in a while and count our blessings."

—Bruce Barton, 1920

SECRET #4:
DARE THEM TO TRAVEL THE UPWARD PATH

"People are what they are; and when you have made up your mind to that you are a long way on the road to serenity."

—Bruce Barton, 1925

THE ZEST OF THE BATTLE

Barton was almost always positive and uplifting in his ads (when he wasn't, the ads often failed) and in his books.

But he knew the value of a challenge.

Barton once suggested that there were two roads in life: one upward, one stuck in monotony. Another of his famous ads (which ran over *seven* years) began,

> "A WONDERFUL TWO YEARS' TRIP
>
> AT FULL PAY—
>
> BUT ONLY MEN WITH IMAGINATION
>
> CAN TAKE IT."

Barton believed the great game of life was to challenge yourself to become the best you could possibly be, whether in business or at home.

He wrote, "Whatever obstacles, whatever disappointments may come, are merely added chances against him, contributing to the zest of the contest."

Barton knew people wanted to improve their lives, but they often didn't act in their own best interest unless prodded. His nudge was a subtle, psychological one.

A 1926 ad for washing machines pointed out that without a machine, your spouse was working for three cents an hour. "Human life is too precious to be sold at a price of three cents an hour," said the ad.

It worked. The reasoning appealed to the desire of people to leave their hardships and troubles behind and begin to move toward an easier, better lifestyle.

Another ad began,

"THIS BOOK MAY NOT BE INTENDED FOR YOU—
BUT THOUSANDS FOUND IN IT WHAT
THEY WERE SEEKING."

And a proposed Campbell's soup ad campaign was to begin with the headline, "Why do you keep on bending over a hot stove to make your own soup?"

Barton challenged readers without insulting them.

There is a fine line here.

If I write an ad that says, "You'd be a fool to pass up my services!" you would probably pass up my services.

But if I write something that begins, "Only the most dedicated achiever will use my services," then you'd probably check out what I had to say. The latter tease would challenge you by subtly asking: "Are you a dedicated achiever?"

Another Barton ad began,

"MEN WHO 'KNOW IT ALL' ARE NOT INVITED
TO READ THIS PAGE!"

I would read that page. Wouldn't you? Why would we read it? Because neither of us is a know-it-all, right?

Again, you're being challenged.

And let's not forget the Marines. They were "looking for a few good men" for decades. It's a challenge that still holds power (and that's why the Marines used the ad).

ONLY YOU SHOULD READ THIS

A friend recently called. She is opening a new business, an antique store, and wanted to know how to use this Barton strategy to get people to attend her grand opening.

"What can I say on my invitation to challenge them to come here?" she asked me.

We kicked around ideas for a moment. Then I offered:

"How about a headline that says, 'Are you one of the few people who can appreciate the value of rare collections?'"

That hit home for her. It clearly challenged people but didn't insult them. We all want to be part of an exclusive group. It appeals to the ego. You just have to be careful not to slap anyone's face with your challenge.

When Barton was brainstorming ideas for the American Tobacco account, he offered this subtle challenge for a radio commercial:

> "We believe that the people who like the finest things—fine books, fine music, fine food—are the people who should like fine tobacco. And if you are one of these people, and if you enjoy this program, and if you have not tried Luckies lately, please buy yourself two packs and smoke them. Really fine tobacco does make a difference in the taste."

And in 1953 Barton advised Schaefer beer to involve its audience. Instead of yelling the company's name, Barton suggested Schaefer become more exciting by tying the beer to popular events, such as baseball games. Barton offered these radio ads: "What are the chances that Joe Black will pitch a no-run game this afternoon?" and "Come over and see whether you think Jackie

Robinson is playing third base as well as he played second."

Do you see how those teasers challenged listeners?

How can you challenge (but not insult) your potential clients and customers?

"Sometimes when I consider what tremendous consequences come from little things . . . I am tempted to think . . . there are no little things."

—Bruce Barton, 1921

"Be genuine. . . . Do not venture into the sunlight unless you are willing first to put your house in order. Emerson said, 'What you are thunders so loud I can't hear what you say.' No dyspeptic can write convincingly of the joys of mincemeat. No woman-hater can write convincingly of love. . . .

"Unless you have a real respect for people, a real affection for people, a real belief that you are equipped to serve them, and that by your growth and prosperity they will likewise grow and prosper, unless you have this deep-down conviction, gentlemen, do not attempt advertising. For somehow it will return to plague you."

—Bruce Barton, 1925

SECRET #5:
THE ONE
ELEMENT MISSING

"I believe the public has a sixth sense of detecting insincerity, and we run a tremendous risk if we try to make other people believe in something we don't believe in. Somehow our sin will find us out."

—Bruce Barton, 1925

DO YOU SUPPORT IT?

Barton's writings had an element that was lacking in most of the other ads of the 1920s through 1940s: sincerity.

Barton's ads came across with a human, inspiring, and friendly feel that people trusted. The secret was Barton's own belief in what he was selling. If he did not support a product or service, he would not write about it. But when he did support it, his honesty came through.

This is an important point with me. Too many people in advertising believe you don't have to care about your product to sell it. They cite stories about John Caples and Maxwell Sackheim writing powerful letters for books they either hadn't read or considered pretty bad.

I disagree.

Who knows how much more powerful the letters Caples and Sackheim wrote could have been had they sincerely loved (or even read) the books they were writing about? It has been my experience that when I support a cause, I can write about it much more powerfully and persuasively. If I don't support it, it shows. Customers aren't stupid.

Besides that, why would you want to sell a product you didn't use or support yourself?

THE ACKNOWLEDGED MASTER

The late John Caples was a master at writing ads. All of his books are classics (and well worth reading).

Who did Caples think was better than himself? Bruce Barton!

Caples said, "Barton had the three things every writer has to have: (1) sincerity, (2) sincerity, (3) sincerity."

Now, the odd thing is that disciples of Caples don't agree that sincerity is necessary. This attitude reeks of peddlers selling magic elixirs. Without sincerity, you're lying to your customers. That's wrong.

One famous copywriter read an early version of this book and said he didn't think sincerity was important, either. He said, "A professional writer should be like a hired assassin. No emotions. Take the product and sell it."

I nearly choked to think this leading authority felt this way about the advertising profession. His attitude reflects what I don't like in business: insincere people out for the buck.

In a sense, however, this copywriter is right. You should be skilled enough to sell anyone a product or service with the power of your words.

But again my point is this: Why would you want to sell a product or service you didn't sincerely endorse?

TRUE SERVICE OR GREED?

Helen Woodward was a cynical but observant business-woman. She was clearly ahead of her time.

Back in 1926 she wrote in *Through Many Windows*, her autobiography, "In the old days, no one ever wrapped money-making eagerness in sweet words like service. Businessmen were frankly after money. They are still after money, but they know now that it is good policy to deliver something good to keep the customer. So they make better goods at better prices—because they have to. And they call that *service*."

Recently a new client came to me. She wanted to write a book on service. When I asked why, she said she had heard it was "in." She had little experience in delivering service and wasn't sure what service really meant, but she was convinced that writing a book on the subject would advance her career. However, it wouldn't advance it far. And not for long.

Without sincerity, you're selling air. Sooner or later someone (a Helen Woodward of our generation) will blow the whistle on you. You'll be exposed as a fraud. You'll lose credibility.

What Woodward saw in her generation was a bunch of businessmen who had heard that service would help them. They weren't sincerely interested in delivering service. They were sincerely interested in making money. (There's nothing wrong with making money; but it should come as a result of your service.)

Roy Durstine (the D in BBDO), in his 1921 book *Making Advertisements and Making Them Pay*, wrote, "Without sincerity an advertisement is no more contagious than a sprained ankle."

And Robert Bedner, in his 1949 senior thesis biography of Barton, wrote, "Contrary to the general belief about advertising men, Barton did regard sincerity and truth as the first essential of successful advertising."

HONESTY SELLS

Barton was sincere. Even Julian Lewis Watkins, while selecting several Barton ads for his book *The 100 Greatest Advertisements*, said Bruce Barton's ads were notable for their sincerity.

Though Barton often had trouble balancing his work life with his spirituality (hence his two most famous books on trying to balance the two), he was earnest. And his honesty showed. It is this characteristic that attracted many people (including me) to his works.

Many studies have shown that the number one element that keeps people from buying anything is lack of trust. Other advertisers have burned them too often before.

You know this is a fact. When you read an ad, you always wonder, "Is this true? Are the claims valid?" This is another reason people read news stories five to nine times more than they read ads. They simply don't trust advertising!

Do you believe in what you are doing or selling? If you don't, you'd better get into something else where your heart and soul can live happily. After all, *you* are the best salesperson for your business! If you aren't convinced, how are you going to excite anyone else?

Bob Bly, the author of 51 business books, says in his *The Copywriter's Handbook*, "When you believe in your product, it's easy to write copy that is sincere, informative, and helpful. And when you are sincere, it comes across to readers and they believe what you've written."

Jay Abraham, a marketing genius who charges over $3,000 an hour for his services, said: "You have to believe in your product. A product has to have a value in your heart and mind before you can passionately translate your enthusiasm to somebody else."

Bruce Barton's genuine feelings for the items or causes he represented helped him create marketing campaigns that broke all earlier records. For example:

- Barton wrote a charity solicitation letter in 1925 that brought in an overwhelming (and previously unheard of) response of well over 100 percent of the goal! His heartfelt letter for Berea College, sent to only 24 people, pulled in over $30,000 in contributions.

- Barton wrote a series of fund-raising letters for Deerfield Academy that were so moving they were collected and sold as examples of sincere writing.

- Barton and Alex Osborn organized the United War Workers Campaign of 1918. Their goal was $175 million. Though the campaign went into effect after World War I ended, the sincerity of the program managed to raise over $204 million—the largest amount ever collected in a freewill offering in the history of the world at that time!

YOU CAN FOOL THEM ONCE (MAYBE)

You can't use the seven secrets in this book to manipulate people into buying from you. This principle of sincerity means people will buy—or not—depending on whether you come across as sincere.

Clyde Bedell, in his 1940 book *How to Write Advertising That Sells*, wrote, "The best way to be sincere is—to be sincere. An attempt to write sincerity into your copy without honestly wanting to be sincere won't work."

When I wrote a sales letter to sell ThoughtLine, an artificial intelligence software program, I was totally in support it of. And my letter showed it. I got an incredible response—over 5 percent—during a recession. (The average sales letter gets no more than 0.02 percent response.)

But when I wrote a letter on another service, one about which I had reservations, my lack of support was seen by all—it was between the lines but still obvious.

That letter was a dud.

You can successfully sell only what you sincerely believe in. You may be able to fool people once, but you'll lose a repeat customer. Since most of your business will come from your satisfied customers (who keep coming back for more), you can't afford to be insincere or manipulative.

Bruce David, author of *Mercenary Marketing*, says if you don't offer a product or service of true value, you won't stay in business. David admits that advertising "may persuade people to try your products or services (as it should) once; but if you don't offer value and quality, you won't convert these people into repeat customers."

THEY TOLD HIM NO

Final thought on this subject: When Bruce Barton wrote his most famous book, *The Man Nobody Knows*, he had no evidence that it would ever sell.

His friends tried to stop him. They said he wasn't an expert. They said there were already far too many books on the subject. They said it would ruin his reputation.

Barton wrote the book because of his sincere desire to share his thoughts. Robert Bedner said, "There is no doubt that the book was written out of sincere conviction."

The result was a best seller in 1925 and 1926 that is still in print today—over 80 years after it was written.

The magic of sincerity.

Do *you* support what you sell or do?

"The advertisements which persuade people to act are written by men who have an abiding respect for the intelligence of their readers, and a deep sincerity regarding the merits of the goods they have to sell."

—Bruce Barton, 1924

Here is Bruce Barton's famous 1925 solicitation letter for Berea College. He sent it to 24 people, hoping to raise $24,000. The result was a response of about $30,000. This is considered one of the most effective letters ever written. See if you can detect how Barton used every one of the strategies in this book when he composed this incredible letter.

Dear Mr. Smith,

For the past three or four years things have been going pretty well at our house. We pay our bills, afford such luxuries as having the children's tonsils out, and still have something in the bank at the end of the year. So far as business is concerned, therefore, I have felt fairly well content.

But there is another side to a man, which every now and then gets restless. It says: "What good are you anyway? What influences have you set up, aside from your business, that would go on working if you were to shuffle off tomorrow?"

Of course, we chip in to the Church and the Salvation Army, and dribble out a little money right along in response to all sorts of appeals. But there isn't much satisfaction in it. For one thing, it's too diffused and, for another, I'm never very sure in my own mind that the thing I'm giving to is worth a hurrah and I don't have time to find out.

A couple of years ago I said: *"I'd like to discover the one place in the United States where a dollar does more net good than anywhere else."* It was a rather thrilling idea, and I went at it in the same spirit in which our advertising agency conducts a market investigation for a manufacturer. Without bothering you with a long story, I believe *I have found the place.*

This letter is being mailed to 23 men besides yourself, 25 of us altogether. I honestly believe that it offers an opportunity to get a maximum amount of satisfaction for a minimum sum.

Let me give you the background.

Among the first comers to this country were some pure-blooded English folks who settled in Virginia but, being more hardy and venturesome than the average, pushed on west and settled in the mountains of Kentucky, Tennessee, North and South Carolina. They were stalwart lads and lassies. They fought the first battle against the British and shed the first blood. In the Revolution they won the battle of King's Mountain. Later, under Andy Jackson, they fought and won the only land victory that we managed to pull off in the War of 1812. Although they lived in southern states they refused to secede in 1860. They broke off from Virginia and formed the state of West Virginia; they kept Kentucky in the Union; and they sent a million men into the northern armies. It is not too much to say that they were the deciding factor in winning the struggle to keep these United States united.

They have had a rotten deal from Fate. There are no roads into the mountains, no trains, no ways of making money. So our prosperity has circled all around them and left them pretty much untouched. They are great folks. The girls are as good-looking as any in the world. Take one of them out of her two-roomed log cabin home, give her a stylish dress and a permanent wave, and she'd be a hit on Fifth Avenue. Take one of the boys, who maybe never saw a railroad train until he was 21, give him a few years of education, and he goes back into the mountains as a teacher or doctor or lawyer or carpenter, and changes the life of a town or county.

This gives you an idea of the raw material. Clean, sound timber—no knots, no wormholes. . . .

Now, away back in the Civil War days, a little college was started in the Kentucky mountains. It started with faith, hope, and sacrifice, and those three virtues are the only endowment it has ever had. Yet today it has accumulated, by little gifts picked up by passing the hat, a plant that takes care of 3,000 students a year. It's the most wonderful manufacturing proposition you ever heard of. They raise their own food, and can it in their own cannery; milk their own cows; make brooms and weave rugs that are sold all over the country; do their own carpentry, painting, printing, horseshoeing, and everything, teaching every boy and girl a trade while he and she are studying. And so efficiently is the job done that—

- A room rents for 60 cents a week (including heat and light).
- Meals are 11 cents apiece (yet all the students gain weight on the fare; every student gets a quart of milk a day).
- The whole cost to a boy or girl for a year's study—room, board, books, etc.—is $146. More than half of this the student earns by work; many students earn all.

One boy walked a hundred miles, leading a cow. He stabled the cow in the village, milked her night and morning, peddled the milk, and put himself through college. He is now a major in the United States Army. His brother, who owned half of the cow, is a missionary in Africa. Seventy-five percent of the graduates go back to the mountains, and their touch is on the mountain counties of five states; better homes, better food, better child health, better churches, better schools; no more feuds; lower death rates.

Now we come to the hook. It costs this college, which is named Berea, $100 a year per student to carry on. She could, of course, turn away 1,500 students each year and break even on the other 1,500. Or she could charge $100 tuition. But then she would be just one more college for the well-to-do. Either plan would be a moral crime. The boys and girls in those one-room and two-room cabins deserve a chance. They are of the same stuff as Lincoln and Daniel Boone and Henry Clay; they are the very best raw material that can be found in the United States.

I have agreed to take ten boys and pay the deficit on their education each year, $1,000. I have agreed to do this if I can get 24 other men who will each take ten. The president, Dr. William J. Hutchins (Yale 1892), who ought to be giving every minute of his time to running the college, is out passing the hat and riding the rails from town to town. He can manage to get $50,000 or $70,000 a year. I want to lift part of his load by turning in $25,000.

This is my proposition to you. Let me pick out ten boys, who are as sure-blooded Americans as your own sons, and just as deserving of a chance. Let me send you their names and tell you in confidence, for we don't want to hurt their pride, where they come from and what they hope to do with their lives. Let me report to you on their progress three times a year. You write me, using the enclosed envelope, that, if and when I get my other 23 men, you will send President Hutchins your check for $1,000. If you will do this I'll promise you the best time you have ever bought for a thousand dollars. Most of the activities to which we give in our lives stop when we stop. But our families go on; and young life goes on and matures and gives birth to other lives. For a thousand dollars a year you can put ten boys or girls back into the mountains who will be a leavening influence in ten towns or counties, and their children will bear the imprint of your influence. Honestly, can you think of any other investment that would keep your life working in the world so long a time after you are gone?

This is a long letter, and I could be writing a piece for the magazines and collecting for it in the time it has taken me to turn it out. So, remember that this is different from any other appeal that ever came to you. Most appeals are made by people who profit from a favorable response, but this appeal is hurting me a lot more than it can possibly hurt you.

What will you have, ten boys or ten girls?

Cordially yours,

Bruce Barton

"Faith in business, faith in the country, faith in one's self, faith in other people—this is the power that moves the world. And why is it unreasonable to believe that this power, which is so much stronger than any other, is merely a fragment of the Great Power which operates the universe?"

—Bruce Barton, *What Can a Man Believe?*, 1927

"I do believe that the one great thing we have got to find a way to do is to make it possible, in our industrial life, for the man who stands at the bench somehow to feel in what he does the same sort of satisfaction and pride which now animates and thrills the man who sits at a desk, and to make the man who stands up to his waist in a ditch, or who swings the ax beside a tree, feel that somehow there is that in the thing he does that reaches down and takes hold on things eternal, and that every swing of the pick and every stroke of the ax is not merely so much servitude, but that, insofar as that is done in a spirit of real pride and satisfaction and service, he makes himself co-worker of Almighty God in the great task of feeding and clothing and housing the world."

—Bruce Barton, 1921 speech

"There is a wise old saying to this effect: 'A great deal of good can be done in the world, if one is not too careful who gets the credit.'

"If your object in life is to get credit, you'll probably get it, if you work hard enough.

"But don't be too much surprised and disappointed when some chap who just went ahead and did the thing, without thinking of the credit, winds up with more medals on his chest than you, with all your striving, have collected on yours."

—Bruce Barton, *It's a Good Old World*, 1920

SECRET #6:
GIVE YOURSELF AWAY

"If a man practices doing things for other people until it becomes so much a habit that he is unconscious of it, all the good forces of the universe line up behind him and whatever he undertakes to do."

—Bruce Barton, 1927

MONEY IS A BY-PRODUCT

Bruce Barton was a great philanthropist.

He devoted time, energy, and money to a wide variety of causes. Some of his best writings were fund-raising letters for colleges and organizations he sincerely believed in.

He also believed in giving something of value away in ads. Most ads contained coupons for a free book. Whatever the item, something has to be given away to start the process of receiving. Giving something away generates credibility. But this strategy also makes the potential customer feel obligated to give something back.

When Barton died in 1967, his estate was worth $2.8 million. But Barton did not spend his life in the pursuit of money. He was quoted as saying that he did what he loved, and the money was a by-product of good work.

That right there may be the greatest secret to prosperity.

Barton wrote, "Get money—but stop once in a while to figure what it is costing you to get it. No man gets it without giving something in return. The wise man gives his labor and ability. The fool gives his life."

SELAH

Barton, a non-Jew, also supported a 1938 organization called Selah that was designed to establish a Jewish state in Baja, California. Though the Mexican government killed that idea, Barton's support of this organization, and many other ones, showed he believed in the power of giving.

A happy by-product of this giving was the fact that it led to business offers, more publicity, and national media exposure, and helped him move into politics.

Again, Barton didn't give in order to get. His giving of time, energy, and money was sincere. But that very giving led to a lot of getting.

WOMEN AND REVOLUTION

Barton supported women's rights long before it was fashionable to do so.

In a 1927 article for *Success* magazine, Barton wrote:

"[Men] have an annoying old idea that strikes me as revolting enough to make any normal woman want to commit murder—i.e., the idea that woman is merely the bearer of children, the leader of the home, the dear sweet good little thing, and after you've said that, that's that!

"Women have a very definite place in the world—the outside world that man has so carefully reserved for himself. I see this great wide sweep of revolution as the most refreshing thing in the century."

Barton's feelings were sincere—even when his feelings were revolutionary.

He wasn't afraid to give his thoughts away in support of something he believed in.

"NO CREDIT, PLEASE"

Barton also wasn't afraid to not get credit for work. It was more important to have the work done than to see that he got the glory for doing it. For example:

Barton was a ghostwriter for leading businessmen, and he wrote at least one speech for President Eisenhower; he wrote many pieces under assumed names (Michael Randall, David Todd, Thomas Ryan, etc.); he let a friend write a play based on his original idea and then shared the authorship; he allowed his loyal secretary of 40 years to edit and rewrite his work; he let his father (a minister) help him think through his religious books; and he let his wife do his shopping (except for books, which he chose himself).

Barton was willing to give away his control. He was willing to delegate. As he once explained in an article, "You can get a lot done if you're not concerned about who gets the credit for it."

ANOTHER LEVEL OF GIVING

"Giving yourself away" also means being vulnerable and honest. Show who you really are—at least reveal enough of your humanness to gain credibility.

Too many businesspeople bark about how wonderful they are. Too many advertisers claim their "amazing" product or service is "the best." Their theory is that your have to sell people, and blowing you own horn is the trick.

Barton knew you could gain the public's trust by letting them know you were human, which means you *may not* be the best, the brightest, or the most amazing.

When I wrote the sales letter to offer this book to my clients and customers, I of course talked about Barton, his ideas, and how the secrets have helped legends throughout history. But I also included a line that said this book isn't a "get rich overnight" book. That one statement made everything else in my letter believable.

When I wrote a sales letter for a software company in California, I told all about the wonders of the software program. But I was certain to include a line that gave away my honesty.

I said, "The program doesn't do your thinking for you, but it does help you think better by joining forces with your own mind."

That one apparently weak point made every other point in my letter believable.

THE FRONT PORCH

Bruce Barton used this secret (and two others) when he wrote a "front porch" interview with Calvin Coolidge, president of the United States in the Roaring Twenties.

The common belief at the time was that people were interested in the politics of politicians. Sounds logical, right? But Barton had a hunch that people were more interested in the *human* qualities of politicians, and especially of the President.

Barton interviewed Coolidge. They spoke of personal interests, family, and other nonpolitical subjects. Barton "revealed the President nobody knows," showed Coolidge's sincerity, and "gave something away"—he gave away the President's mask of power.

The newspaper reports of the day were jealous and angry. They wanted a different story. But the public—the voters—loved it.

Earnest Elmo Calkins, another pioneer in advertising, wrote:

> "The public was more deeply moved to learn how the President did his shopping, or that when he was up home in the country he liked to putter around and fix the lock on the woodshed door, exactly as you or I, than to learn his views on Farm Relief or the World Court. In short, they were more interested in the President as a human being than as a politician or a statesman."

Bruce Barton's historic interview simply "gave something away" to the people: humanness.

HOW GIVING LED TO GREATNESS

Batten, Barton, Durstine, & Osborn (BBDO), once the largest ad agency in the world (named Agency of the Year in 2005 by *Adweek* and *Advertising Age* magazines), began as a result of this very secret.

Starting in 1918, at the end of World War I, Bruce Barton donated his talents to the United War Workers Campaign. He also helped promote various charities, including the Salvation Army (Barton coined its famous slogan, "A man may be down but he's never out").

It was during this work that Barton met Alex Osborn and Roy Durstine (The O and D in BBDO). They became friends. Osborn persuaded Barton to form an agency with Durstine. On January 2, 1919, the agency of Barton and Durstine opened with 14 employees.

In August of the same year Osborn joined the firm. By 1925 BDO was the fifth largest ad firm in the country. In 1928 the firm merged with the George Batten Company and became BBDO, with Bruce Barton as president.

And this now-legendary advertising agency, with offices all over the world and thousands of employees, began from an act of charity!

If Bruce Barton had not contributed his time and energy to the United War Workers Campaign, if he had not given himself away for a cause he sincerely believed in, the BBDO agency might never have been created.

TOP THIS

Bruce Barton gave himself away to a staggering roster of worthy causes—and this is not a complete list!

- National chairman, United Negro College Fund
- Publicity committee, National Urban League
- National chairman, American Heart Association
- Public relations committee, Salvation Army
- Fund-raising, Deerfield Academy
- President, Institute for the Crippled and Disabled
- Fund-raising, Berea College

What are *you* giving?

"Until a man is old enough to lose the idea that the purpose of life is self-entertainment, until he quits trying to entertain himself and begins trying to entertain other people, he is bound to be restless and unhappy. You must forget yourself in order to please yourself."

—Bruce Barton, *On the Up and Up*, 1929

"Say to yourself: 'Here I am, a human being just a little different from any who has ever lived before or will ever live again. I don't have 100 percent equipment by any means. There are some notable lacks in my make-up, and no notable points of strength. But this is the hand that has been dealt me in the game, and I must play it. And I shall be judged not by what I accomplish in contrast with other men, but by what I make of myself in comparison with what I might have made."

—Bruce Barton, 1921

"The greatest educational force in modern life is advertising.

"I said to this country doctor, 'There are five of you doctors in town; how much do you make?' He said, 'Two are starving and the other three are just barely getting along.' I said, 'Is there any cooperation among you?'

"He said, 'Not on your life. I hardly dare to take a vacation, because I am afraid the other doctors will steal my customers.' I said, 'If you would join together, spend a little money every week on advertising, if you would sell this community on the necessity of having an annual or semiannual examination, if you would sell the community on the importance of having proper dental care in the schools and having regular health supervision of the children in the schools, you would all make more money and the community would be immeasurably in your debt.'"

—Bruce Barton, in *Masters of Advertising Copy*, 1925

SECRET #7: SHARPEN THE KNIFE

"When we are through changing—we are through."
—Bruce Barton, 1921

SPIT POLISHED

Everything Barton wrote was polished to perfection. He knew you had to "sharpen the knife" of persuasion by rewriting, testing, getting feedback, and being flexible.

During the 1930s, when Barton's name was a household word and businesspeople were lining up at the door of BBDO to have the famous writer do their ads, Barton was wise enough to get help. He wrote many ads himself. Many others were done by the other "Bruce Bartons" hired to do the work. Yet the real Barton always supervised and revised every word until the ad was honed to perfection.

Why?

Because Barton knew that your best work comes after you've revised it. The great literary stylist E. B. White said there was no great writing, only great rewriting.

Barton once wrote that most writers start writing something before they start *saying* something. Editing is your opportunity to be sure what you've created is irresistible.

In 1920 Barton said Horace Greeley, the legendary newspaperman, used to say that "the way to write a good editorial was to write it to the best of your ability, then cut it in two in the middle and print the last half."

Most of the great advertising giants from the Roaring Twenties and beyond knew it was wiser to create 25 headlines before settling on one. (Barton actually often created *over 100 headlines* and selected one from the list.)

The great admen often wrote several different ads before deciding which would work best. They all knew the value of this secret—honing your work until it was perfect.

MAKE IT TIGHT

Barton was no exception. It's said that he was a stickler when it came to writing. He always wanted the copy tight. A running joke was that when he died his headstone would say, "The copy should be shorter."

Simplify and tighten your ads, your talks, your letters, and your meetings, until they squeak with tense power. Brevity is the key.

"Two men spoke at Gettysburg on the same afternoon during the Civil War," Barton wrote in 1920. "One man— the leading orator of his day—made a 'great' oration—

"The other speaker read from a slip of paper less than 300 words. His speech—Lincoln's Gettysburg Address— will live forever."

Even Lincoln knew the power of a few well-chiseled words.

SMART ADS

Far too many businesspeople admire seemingly creative ads rather than asking if the ads pull in business. Cuteness and cleverness do not usually work.

The 1991 ads for Isuzu automobiles are a perfect example. The ads won awards for their humor and originality. But did they sell cars? No. Isuzu was often dead last in terms of car sales.

Your focus should be on ads that work—on ads that get the results you want. That happens when you "sharpen the knife" of persuasion.

People usually ask themselves (unconsciously) three basic questions when they look at ads: "Who cares? So what? What's in it for me?"

When I was working on a title for this book, I thought I'd call it *The Secrets of Bruce Barton*. But people would say, "Who cares?" because they wouldn't recall Barton.

Then I thought I'd try *The Strategies of a Forgotten Ad Man*. But people would say, "What's in it for me?"

I also thought I'd title the book *Bruce Barton: A Biography*. But people would say, "So what?" since they wouldn't know who Barton was.

The current title speaks to what people want. By sharpening the knife I was able to come up with a much stronger title.

Bruce Barton once told this story about sharpening the knife to make an advertisement more powerful:

"The human being from Adam's day to the present has been interested first of all and most of all in himself. My firm once took over the advertising of a life insurance company and has handled it now for many years. When we took it over every insurance man would tell you that the strongest appeal you could make in insurance would be to show the picture of an attractive young widow with a couple of pretty children at her knee and the photograph of her deceased husband in her hand—with some headline as 'Wasn't daddy wonderful to take out life insurance to protect us?'

"We began using that appeal but soon found that there was a much stronger appeal. We cut the widow and children out of the illustrations; instead we showed a happy-faced man of 65 sitting on a rock, with a brier pipe in his mouth and an old felt hat on his head, saying: 'He doesn't have to do a lick of work, and every month gets the check for $200.'

"The self-interest appeal (the desire to enjoy life and live longer) out-pulled the wife and child appeal by about 10 to 1."

HEALING KNIVES

Since the image of a knife may cause you to shudder, let me tell you why I'm using it.

A knife can cut. A knife can kill. But a knife can also heal. Surgeons use knives to help you live.

"Sharpen the knife" doesn't mean to get ready to maim your customers. It means get read to *serve* your customers by sharpening your advertisements and marketing strategies so they do what you want them to do: bring in new business.

SHARPEN YOUR CHOICES

This strategy is also a reminder to sharpen our decisions.

I play the harmonica. Though I'm not Charlie Musslewhite or Howard Levy, I'm not bad, either. I play in a band from time to time, and I practice with friends.

Sounds innocent enough, doesn't it?

But I've noticed some problems.

Trying to devote my life to being an author and to being a musician is nearly impossible. Both careers require time and commitment. And neither allow for sideline activities. If I try to do both, I do neither very well.

On the days I try to write after staying up the night before playing music, I'm a flop. I can't get anything done. My head is too fuzzy. And on the evenings when I try to blow my harp after writing and seeing clients all day, I'm too tired to hit the right note.

Hobbies and relaxing pastimes are fine. But trying to chase two massive dreams isn't smart. Bruce Barton was the first to help me realize I had to sharpen my decisions. In 1920 he wrote an essay called "Slide Lines," which ended as follows:

"J.C. Penney told me the other day about a young man who might have been one of his first partners. The young man played the trombone and was compelled to leave the store early every night because he made five dollars a week by tooting his horn in an orchestra. He is still tending store in the daytime and tooting at night. Mr. Penney is the head of more than eight hundred stores.

"There are men who have made fortunes by running boot-black stands, by buying junk from automobile factories, and even by contracting with a city to collect its garbage.

Almost any business seems to be a good business if a man gives it all he's got.

"But the side line is the slide line."

ACT BEFORE IT'S TOO LATE

This strategy also refers to your life.

It was the July 1, 1991, death of actor Michael Landon that drove this point home for me. His sudden passing made me aware that you have to do what you know to do *now*—today—before it's too late. Our time here is limited. Landon was one of the most robust people I've ever seen. He was strong and healthy and full of life. But that didn't make him immune to dying.

Bruce Barton's life roared during the 1920s through 1950s. He was healthy and alive. But he lost a son, a daughter, and a wife. He had a stroke. And by 1967, the year of his death at age 80, illness had wiped out his memory. Nearly helpless, he died alone except for a few friends and relatives.

If Barton had not written the books he did, when he did, our world would have suffered an incalculable loss. If Michael Landon had not written and starred in the shows he did, our lives would have a mysterious hole in them.

"Sharpening the knife" is a strategy that applies to you personally. This book may have prompted some ideas in you. Are you going to take action? Are you going to do what you know to do?

If you knew your work would touch people in the same way as the work of Bruce Barton or Michael Landon, would you act today?

Bruce Barton wrote, "It's only when we are stirred by a great demand, an insistent necessity, that we accomplish the sort of things that make us proud of our humanity."

That demand has to come from you. *You* have to sharpen the knife of your own being. Runners call it exceeding your personal best. Instead of competing against anyone, you run to improve yourself, to better your previous time.

Are you "sharpening the knife" that is you?

"If you are going to do anything you must expect criticism. But it's better to be a doer than a critic. The doer moves; the critic stands still, and is passed by.

"You must believe in something—in yourself, in the country, in God. You must have courage to back that belief with your money and your life, and patience to wait for fulfillment."

—Bruce Barton, 1932

INSTANT ACCESS
TO THE SEVEN
LOST SECRETS

THE FIRST SECRET: REVEAL THE BUSINESS NOBODY KNOWS

What are you *really* in the business of delivering? What universal need are you fulfilling? Look past the obvious.

THE SECOND SECRET: USE A GOD TO LEAD THEM

Can you establish yourself as an expert in your field? Can you write a book about your service?

THE THIRD SECRET: SPEAK IN PARABLES

What are your stories? Who has bought from you and prospered or changed? Learn to use "story selling" methods.

THE FOURTH SECRET: DARE THEM TO TRAVEL THE UPWARD PATH

How can you challenge your customers without insulting them? Think of the Marines.

THE FIFTH SECRET: THE ONE
ELEMENT MISSING

Do you sincerely believe in what you are doing and sell-ing? If not, why not?

THE SIXTH SECRET: GIVE YOURSELF AWAY

What are you giving to your clients? To the world?

THE SEVENTH SECRET: SHARPEN THE KNIFE

Are you polishing your writings, your ads, until they are perfect? Go for effectiveness rather than cleverness. Are you polishing yourself?

SPECIAL REPORT: ANALYSIS OF BRUCE BARTON'S 100 PERCENT RESPONSE LETTER

Maverick marketer Craig Perrine and I analyzed the famous Bruce Barton letter that pulled a better than 100 percent response. (The letter appears in Chapter 5.) This lively and eye-opening discussion reveals many points to help you write better sales pieces of your own.

IMAGINE WHAT WILL HAPPEN TO YOUR BUSINESS ONCE YOU LEARN THE SECRETS BEHIND THE SUCCESS OF THE HISTORIC SALES LETTER THAT COMMANDED A 100 PERCENT RESPONSE!

Joe: Hi and welcome. This is Dr. Joe Vitale. . . . I'm very excited because I have a guest here who is going to help me along in investigating one of the greatest sales letters of all time. It was a fund-raising letter, written by Bruce Barton in 1925. This letter—brace yourself—got a 100 percent response. I'm pausing for dramatic emphasis here because 100 percent is not only impressive, it's probably miraculous. That is incredible. Most letters, as you probably know, get a 2 percent to 5 percent response, depending on the letter, the audience, and who it's going to. It can go higher. It can be 30 percent or even 50 percent; but a 100 percent letter! We all know that people move, people die, or people are not interested in buying the same products and services again. So, to get a 100 percent response is pretty darn historic, legendary, and amazing. And this letter was done in 1925, sent by Bruce Barton.

Now let's look at Bruce Barton for a second. Bruce Barton was a founder of one of the largest advertising agencies in the world, BBDO. It's still around today. BBDO stands for Batten, Barton, Durstine, & Osborn. They were the four gents who started it back in 1919. It quickly became a powerhouse of an advertising agency.

Bruce Barton was probably the most famous of the four during that period. He was a best-selling author. He wrote a book called *The Man Nobody Knows*, which is still in print. He wrote many sales letters, many articles, and many fund-raising letters. He was considered a business celebrity. . . .

This letter is an example of one of his techniques, a technique that I call sincerity. It was sent to 24 people and got a 100 percent response. Now, the first thing people say when they hear that is, "Oh, it was sent to only 24 people. Of course he got a 100 percent response." And I think that's a ridiculous view. That's low-level thinking, because you can't even send out 24 Christmas cards and get 24 Christmas cards back these days.

He was sending out 24 letters and asking people to give $1,000 each. Now remember, this was 1925. So, asking for $1,000 at that point might have been the equivalent of asking for $50,000 or probably even much more today. So, it's a tough thing to ask for, any way you look at it. He asked for it with this letter, and he got it.

Now, I'm not by myself, as I've already mentioned. I've got help here with me to go through this letter—the famous or infamous Craig Perrine of ListProfitSecrets. com. Thanks for making time to be here, Craig.

Craig: Joe, thank you very much. It's an honor to discuss this with you and go over such a fabulously successful letter.

Joe: You've talked about this letter before, so I already know you like it. . . . We're going to dissect it. Read a little bit of it as we comment on it. So, we'll bring it all to life for you, and what we're looking for is, in short, what makes this work.

Why does this letter work? So, unless you have something to add to that, Craig, I'm ready to jump into this thing.

Craig: Well, I think we should just jump right in.

Joe: Okay, I want to make a brief acknowledgment. This is all being recorded by Pat O'Bryan of patobryan.com, who is sitting to my left, quietly recording everything, smiling, nodding his head when we say things that are wise and wonderful, and grimacing if we don't. So anyway, let's begin here.

This letter begins with "Dear Mr. Smith." Now, of course, he personalized it with everybody, and I want to stop right there because the average letter has a big, bold headline on it. And you hear copywriters and direct marketers say all the time you have to have a headline on your letter. This letter does not have a headline on it. I thought about that and my first response, and I want to hear what you have to say, Craig.

My first response was we use a headline only when we are trying to get people to pay attention to the letter. We're using a headline to give them a reason to read the letter. We use a headline because we don't know their first name or we don't know what's going to actually pull them into it. But if we know their first name, we can say "Dear Joe" or "Dear Craig" or "Dear Pat" or whoever it happens to be. We don't need the headline. The person's name alone is going to be so powerful that they will at least begin the letter.

Another thing that's going on here is that this letter came from Bruce Barton, who, as I've already said, was pretty well known and probably everybody who got this letter knew him personally or knew of him. So, that was the second reason they would begin the letter—and remember, only begin the letter. And it's also the reason why they might not need a headline.

So, again it's coming from Bruce Barton. If it's coming from somebody that they already know, the headline may not be necessary, and if they are using their first name—in other words, making the letter very personal—you may not need the headline. So in this case, it's a personal letter from a well-known person. No headline is needed.

Craig: I think another thing that's really great about this and a disarming quality of not having a headline is that it immediately takes it out of the realm of the sales letter. And if you look at what he does with it later, I think that's an inherent part of his approach here; that if he had started out with "How to do anything," "Do it now," or "Read this," it would have had an entirely different setup to the letter, but, I think, it would have had an undesirable effect given what he did later on.

So, I can't read his mind, of course, but I think it's a perfect way to set up; this is a personal letter from me to you, and that immediately will grant me a higher response than if it's just an ad.

Joe: Yeah, I love that observation. Obviously, we don't even know what he wants at this point, so we have to start reading the letter. It has a couple of things going for it, of course. In this case, no headline is wonderful because the headline is the opening: "Dear Mr. Smith." That's the headline. So, we go right into the first paragraph, which I love because it says, "For the past three or four years things have been going pretty well at our house. We pay our bills, afford such luxuries as having the children's tonsils out, and still have something in the bank at the end of the year. So far as business is concerned, therefore, I have felt fairly well content." And I like that because not only is this personal, it's sincere. It is also still playing the curiosity card a little bit because we don't know what he's writing to us about. If everything is going okay, why the letter? But there's a hint of dissatisfaction in the very few lines that begin this letter, because when he says, "So far as business is concerned, therefore, I have felt fairly well content," he's implying that he is not content in some other area. And I love this because it's very subtle.

It's kind of going underneath the radar. It's stirring up that curiosity, and I love curiosity. Curiosity is one of the most hypnotic, powerful motivators we can ever play, and he's playing it heavily but in such a low-key kind of way that you can barely see it. But you start reading this opening paragraph, just the first couple of lines, and you are going, "Yep, that sounds great, wonderful." I also think as a side note that it's so ironic: 1925 is during the party years. We are in the Roaring Twenties. People are doing pretty well and they don't see 1929 coming. They don't see the Great Depression coming, and from a historical vantage point looking back, it's like "Oh, man, if they only knew."

Craig: Right. They probably would have kept their thousand dollars.

Joe: If I could have only gone back and said, "Oh, hold onto some money or invest differently or don't buy stocks, especially around October 1929." But again, this is 1925.

Anything else that you notice in those opening lines?

Craig: Well, it is exactly what you said. I love that part—the sudden, indirect nature, and it really sets the tone for the closing paragraph, which of course we'll get to. Well, he is hinting that there is something missing from all of this material and financial success. Getting the tonsils out probably in those days was a much more expensive, complicated procedure than it is today, so that may not resonate the same way today with us as it did then. But he's matching with his audience the sentiments and feelings that they probably also have, since he knows his audience.

This was targeted to 24 very specific people. So, he knows and he's going right for a target that we'll see develop later in the letter. But it's a perfect opening, and yes, it's very indirect, and I think that's a reason it's similar to not having a headline. Also, the opening paragraph isn't direct, right for the jugular (in fact, it is, though, in an indirect way).

Joe: In an indirect way, which is the beautiful part of the psychology behind the letter. Now, this next paragraph fascinates me because he says, "But there is another side to a man, which every now and then gets restless. It says: 'What good are you anyway? What influences have you set up, aside from your business, that would go on working if you were to shuffle off tomorrow?'"

And I love this because in a way he's mind reading, but what he's doing is creating rapport. He's merging with what people are already thinking.

This is one of the techniques that Robert Collier and the famous Robert Collier letter book talks about—something like "getting on the same train that your reader is on" so that you're going in that direction to begin with. In hypnotic terms, you're merging with their cultural trance. So he's beginning that by saying, "But there is another side to a man, which every now and then gets restless." We're all going, "Yes! I know what you are talking about, Bruce. I understand right where you are coming from. I feel that way."

And then when he asks, "What good are you any-way?," all of these people at some point or other, includ-ing us, are moved. People have told me they read this letter today, and they want to give money to Berea College—that's powerful. And part of the reason for what's going on is that they are creating this rapport. Bruce is saying, "Yes, I know what you are thinking," without actually saying it.

He goes on with the next paragraph and says, "Of course, we chip in to the Church and the Salvation Army, and dribble out a little money right along in response to all sorts of appeals." Then he says, "But there isn't much satisfaction in it. For one thing, it's too diffused and, for another, I'm never very sure in my own mind that the thing I'm giving to is worth a hurrah and I don't have time to find out." I swear, Craig, I have thought that very same thing. I have given to this, that, and the other cause, and done the same questioning process.

I've wondered, well, if I give $50 or $5,000 or $50,000, does that really make a dent in what needs to be done in the world? And even if I give that amount, how do I know that it's going to be used in the way that I would intend for it to be used? So Bruce is really reading my mind, even today. This letter is from 1925. We are in 2007. I'm reading this letter and I can say, yeah, if he sent this letter to me right now, I'd be nodding my head and saying, "Bruce, I'm thinking the same thing. I'm wondering the same thing."

So this is deepening that whole level of rapport with the reader. He's merging with what the reader is already asking on their own level, inside their mind, right down to the next paragraph: "A couple of years ago I said: *'I'd like to discover the one place in the United States where a dollar does more net good than anywhere else.'* It was a rather thrilling idea, and I went at it in the same spirit in which our advertising agency conducts a market investigation for a manufacturer. Without bothering you with a long story, I believe *I have found the place.*" This is a turning point in the letter. I can get really excited, so be sure to interrupt me and tell me what you are thinking, Craig, because this is so psychologically fascinating.

Craig: It's just pure genius, of course, which is not surprising, given who wrote it. But if you look at that paragraph that we started with here, where he's saying, "But there is another side to a man," that's a very definitive statement. And one of the other things that I think is going on there is that he's taken a dominant role. He's telling the reader how life is, that there is another side to a man. He could say, "Well, don't you think" or "Is there possibly."

He's telling you that there is, and what he's doing here is setting up, first of all, a dominant relationship where he's going to be telling you what to do at the end of the letter. But he's also doing it indirectly because he couldn't say, "Hey, Mr. Smith, by the way, what really are you worth anyway? What good have you done?" You can't say that directly. And yet, as you pointed out, in the next line where he is talking about the one place where a dollar goes further and all these sorts of things, he has talked about the objections to ordinary charity, where you don't know how effective it is.

He's already countering objections you don't even know you are going to raise, because you don't know why he's writing yet—even now.

Joe: Brilliant insight. I hadn't even picked up on all of that. So, that's brilliant. One thing that I didn't pick up on that's in this fourth paragraph is where he says, "It was a rather thrilling idea, and I went at it in the same spirit in which our" (notice) "advertising agency conducts a market investigation for a manufacturer." That is rebuilding his position of authority here. It's also a very subtle reminder: "By the way, I started BBDO. We are a giant advertising agency. We can do all kinds of market research."

He doesn't have to brag. He doesn't have to spell all of that out. He just very calmly mentions that "our advertising agency conducts a market investigation for a manufacturer." So, he's mentioning this, which also increases his ego-dominance, if you will. Not in a negative way. This is a positioning. It's a mental positioning, and then he's also pointing out that he thoroughly investigated this whole fund-raising aspect at the same level, the same kind of depth that his company would do if they were doing market campaign research.

So, he is saying that this is not a wispy, lighthearted investigation. He is leading up to something big here. And within four paragraphs he's paved the way to go right into your brain. You talk about a hypnotic letter and a hypnotist—I don't know if Bruce Barton ever studied hypnosis, but there are a lot of elements of hypnotic commands going on in here. So, I'm fascinated by this. He goes on to begin to explain what this letter is all about.

"This letter is being mailed to 23 men besides yourself, 25 of us altogether." Now this is very powerful. As soon as you read this and you realize, "Oh, I'm one of 25," you're in a special crowd. You are now separate from the mass of humanity. You are one of the hand-chosen ones. You know, I'd think that he had been studying too much Christianity if he had said something like "You are one of 12 people who have gotten this." You'd know that he was going to start a movement! But you are one of 25, and it's the same kind of philosophy that's going on or psychological play that's going on.

Suddenly you feel like this letter is a special letter and you are a special person. You've received it from this well-known person (as he has already reminded us, he has his own advertising agency). You know that he's got a name for himself. This is something that you need to read. At this point, you are really locked in.

Craig: And by leveling the playing field there with "I've done this investigation," he's already removed the objection of "How well have you thought this out? Is this for real? How serious is this?" And when he said "another side to a man," he set up perhaps a need that they feel. They may not have had it on their minds immediately, but something's missing. There is a problem. You don't have an outlet for your charitable giving. That means as much as what he's setting up here.

And then when it gets down to here, what he's done is he's going to start giving you the solution. But he created the problem in your mind by setting it up first.

Joe: Beautiful, beautiful insight. I like this next line. It's one line, all by itself, a beautiful statement. "Let me give you the background." This is the beginning of a story, and as everybody should know, stories are one of the most powerful vehicles for getting a message across. It's a way to get under a person's mental radar. It's a way to get your message across without people filtering it out. It's going in below their conscious awareness in a lot of ways.

But this is almost saying, "Pull up chair. Make yourself a cup of tea. I'm going to put my arm around you. Let's put our feet up and let me tell you this story." And it just says, "Let me give you the background."

Craig: And the funny thing is he already has been giving them the background. He's been setting them up with, "There's something you're missing, I'm going to tell you exactly what that missing thing is. I've already done all the research. You are one of a few select people who even know about this, and now let's get into the other background."

Joe: Wow, that's a good reminder, because he did all of that in six paragraphs. So, when people think that you have to write really long copy to get people involved, no, that's not the case. You may have to write long copy to complete your message and to get to the close, to the sale, to finish the persuasion; but these six paragraphs pave the way to lock somebody in to read this entire letter. And as I pointed out, there are people who read this letter today who go online looking for Berea College, which is still around, wanting to give money because of this sales letter. That's how powerful it is.

Craig: Another thing: In traditional copywriting a lot of advice says that you start out with a promise. You open up with a problem. You say something very direct that will give your reader an indication of "what's in it for me." And I want to again underscore that that's not really explicit here. Everything is indirect. Two things about that: First of all, his audience that he was gearing toward were very successful men and they had a lot of money and so on. He's not going to talk to them about how they can make more money.

Looking at Maslow's Hierarchy of Needs, he's not going to talk to them about how they can meet some of the lower needs. He's talking about self-actualization and how to have them contribute and do things like that. It's a more high-minded type of need that they do feel because it's what's missing at their level. So, he's writing at their level but he also knows, probably being a successful man himself, that they are also pitched a lot and asked for money.

Joe: I'm glad you said that.

Craig: So, he's doing this, and we don't know what he's asking for yet. We've already had all these levels of meaning given and now the background, the story, is coming, but he hasn't asked for anything yet. And it's all indirect and I think that is a wonderful example for today when everyone is so desensitized by massive amounts of advertising that I believe there is a definite time and place to use an indirect approach like this.

Joe: This is beautiful. Well, you also pointed out that he kept his audience in mind. Now this is going to be true for every letter that we write. You want to keep the audience in mind, the people who are going to be receiving the letter. You want to speak to them in their language and keep their concerns in mind. What's on their mind as you begin writing to them? When they receive your letter, what are they already thinking? And you want to merge with that to the best of your ability. . . .

Bruce knew all of that. This is a brilliant letter, and it's only the beginning of it. So, we are going to see if we can get through some more of it. He's going to begin giving you the background. And of course he leads into this story, beginning with, "Among the first comers to this country were some pure-blooded English folks who settled in Virginia but, being more hardy and venturesome than the average, pushed on west and settled in the mountains of Kentucky, Tennessee, North and South Carolina."

He's telling a story here, and as we all know, stories are incredibly captivating. He's revealing some of the problems as he goes into the story because he begins the next paragraph by saying, "They have had a rotten deal from Fate." Uh-oh, what was the rotten deal? There's a problem here. "There are no roads into the mountains, no trains, no ways of making money. So our prosperity has circled all around them and left them pretty much untouched." I love this because he's also playing the emotion card.

Suddenly, we're doing fine. We're experiencing prosperity. We can afford to get the kids' tonsils out and all the things that he played up in the beginning. We can afford to have our own advertising agency and so forth, but prosperity—I love even the wording here: "Our prosperity has circled all around them and left them pretty much untouched." This is emotion. He's playing on our emotions. Soon, he's going to get into the logic of this, which I love. There's a balance in this letter of emotion and logic, but he's revealing a problem as he's telling all of this.

Craig: Well, he's creating a sense of "you have a lot, these folks don't." And one of the things that's coming through here is—I wouldn't say guilt directly—but there is a sense where you have empathy and you feel like on the scale you have a lot, and you are now feeling like "Wow, I have empathy for these folks. I understand historical reality and why they are poor and uneducated." He actually is countering potential prejudice that you might have of all of those "inborn, inbred West Virginia hill people." Here he is saying, essentially, that they are just like us. Circumstances—they are off in some geographically isolated area—no blame. They are not ignorant. They are doing everything they can with the harsh limitations of what's around them and therefore, by the way, are poor and uneducated through no fault of their own.

So, I think he's speaking to his audience about potential class differences there. And he's just removing all that and saying, we're all people here and there's something, remember, that a man has to ask himself: "What good am I anyway?"

Joe: Exactly.

Craig: And so, this is all said beautifully and we still don't know what he wants.

Joe: Beautiful observation. We're partway through, and we still don't know what he wants. He's setting this up. It's like this great chess game here and he's moving all the pieces before we get our move. So, I love how Bruce is telling a story throughout this letter. And he's building up emotion. He's building up curiosity. He's building up even some enthusiasm. And as you pointed out, Craig, we still don't even know what he really wants at this point, which is also keeping us reading because we don't know.

What does Bruce want? He has merged with our thinking. We understand that there's a rapport going on. We understand there's a story being told, a very interesting story. But what does he want? He even goes on, after telling this story, which really involves the emotion. Going the way back with the paragraph that begins, "Now, away back in the Civil War days, a little college was started in the Kentucky mountains." Doesn't he even sound like a storyteller at that point? It's like a story, and he is a grand storyteller. He's a famous author.

He's written many best-selling books. It's not just *The Man Nobody Knows* but many other books. And he says, "It started with faith, hope, and sacrifice," which all sounds wonderful, "and those three virtues are the only endowment it has ever had." Now this sounds even noble. This sounds like it's beyond a human duty. These people are going with almost beyond human capabilities to accomplish something with the bare minimum of anything and certainly without any prosperity. But all of this is just telling a story to get the emotion going.

Suddenly we start moving into what I'm seeing as the logic. He starts moving into the paragraph where it says, "a room rents for 60 cents a week (including heat and light)," this is where he begins with the sentence that says, "And so efficiently is the job done that—a room rents for 60 cents a week (including heat and light); meals are 11 cents apiece (yet all the students gain weight on the fare; every student gets a quart of milk a day). The whole cost to a boy or girl for a year's study—room, board, books, etc.—is $146." Wow, that was 1925. This is pretty amazing.

"More than half of this the student earns by work; many students earn all. One boy walked a hundred miles, leading a cow. He stabled the cow in the village, milked her night and morning, peddled the milk, and put himself through college. He is now a major in the United States Army. His brother, who owned half the cow, is a missionary in Africa." These are wonderful stories that are communicating to you some of the things without him directly saying them.

You are finding out that these people are working very hard, that they are becoming successful, that they are paying their own way, that they are not asking for handouts, and that the money that they do get is not being wasted. All of this is very logical. And it's all part of the story. He's painting a very complete picture.

Craig: He's also laying essentially the groundwork for one of the most persistent and inspiring plot themes in fiction—sort of a hero overcoming obstacles.

Joe: Yes!

Craig: And what you're buying into at some level when you read this is you want to have a happy ending. You want them to succeed, and at the end when the close to the letter comes around, you're going to find that you are a part of helping them succeed and you can actually help make the outcome. And I'm fairly sure that it's not an accident that that's how it works out.

Joe: You end up being a hero, too. Well, I love how this moves along at a pretty quick pace. Even though this is a long letter, you notice that it becomes very captivating as you keep reading it and becomes more involved, again with the story, again with the subtleness of it and the psychological workings behind it. Then we get to the line where it says, "Now we come to the hook." He hasn't quite told us what he wants yet, but we're starting to get closer and you can almost guess what he wants when we start to read this

"It costs this college, which is named Berea," (well, finally we even know what the college's name is—it's Berea) "$100 a year per student to carry on. She could, of course, . . ." Now, I want to stop there. He called this college "she." I can't help but think that was relevant. He didn't say "the college," "it," or "he." He called it "she," and I think that was tapping into the feminine, a mothering instinct.

He was, of course, giving the college life. You know, it wasn't just one thing or another. This was a she. This was a woman. It was a living being. I found that relevant. Did it mean anything to you?

Craig: Well, it had struck me as his playing to the damsel in distress, hero rides to the rescue type of theme.

To go back to where you were talking about what charities to give to and looking for a valid one and all that, by giving all the specific prices and costs for everything, he's also underscoring "we did a lot of research here." He's not saying, "Oh, let's just chuck some money at this and hopefully it will work out." He's actually displaying proof here and showing you that in truth, every dollar does count in this environment. Sixty cents—he's giving very specific amounts so that again at the end, you don't have any questions about, "Well, what's this money for and how is it allocated and what does it really cost to run this and to succeed," as he's setting it up.

But yes, I do think that's setting up that these are all men he's addressing. So, there's no gender confusion. I think the "she" is definitely a brilliant stroke there. And I also like how he says, "Now we come to the hook." Because you also can't hide that they know at some point they are going to get hit up for something, and here he is being very honest about that. And that disarms them because they don't feel like it's a game. Okay, he's going to ask now. And he's stating he's going to ask. And here's a hook. He's even calling it a hook. So, I think when you are up-front and honest like that, it removes the pressure of being suspicious and looking for the hook.

Joe: Well, I think I should point out that I put this letter in the chapter about the lost secret that's called "sincerity" because this letter reeks of sincerity. And I think that sincerity needs to be in all the letters that we send out—not just a fund-raising letter but in all of them—the personal letters, the e-mails, the sales letters, everything that you can think of. This letter is very sincere, and of course he's taking away every objection that you could have before you even have it in this case.

Now, people like Dan Kennedy say one of the best ways to write a sales letter is to list all the reasons why somebody will not buy from you. Think of every possible reason why they will object and not buy whatever it is you are asking for, and answer every one of those in your sales letter. Of course, a clumsy way of doing that is to just list the question or the objection and your answer to it.

But in a masterful way, you do it like Bruce Barton here; you weave this story and you talk about what's going on without even getting to the hook until we are at the point where he's already taken away just about every objection that we might have. And again, we're not quite sure what he's going to ask of us yet, but he's already in our head, playing with our mind in a very hypnotic way.

Craig: The funny thing is the hook was really in the second paragraph, and again with the "Let me give you the background." He's telling you, essentially, he's positioning the flag here. "Now I'm going to tell you the hook," when, in point of fact, every paragraph has had a hook in it that has kept you in the process and got you emotionally involved. And if you're going to ask anybody for money or for a sale or for anything, it always is going to amount to the fact that they need to trust that you are going to deliver or that they are going to get whatever it is you are promising. And if you deal with the objections in this indirect way, before they even have them, their minds are almost defenseless in the sense that they don't have anything to object to. They are already sort of a check box: "Yep, that's okay," "Oh, well, I agree with that." "Of course, who could argue with that?" "Of course, look at these virtuous people." And now he's going to present them—defenseless—with the hook that they've already been experiencing.

Joe: Which is beautiful. This letter is well worth the study. Let me pause and give people a tip on one of the ways to integrate the hidden mechanisms behind this letter, because there is probably going to be a lot that I don't even see and you may not see and we certainly can't cover in this short time that we have together. So I would suggest taking this letter and writing it out by hand, not typing it into your computer, though you can do that. But I would take a piece of paper and a pen and write this letter out, word for word, because when you start to do that, you start to make conscious some of the things that are unconscious even to us as we are reading and talking about this letter.

We are trying to dissect it right here but (and I haven't done this exercise) I just know that it would be very powerful for me to sit down and write this letter out word for word, and pay attention to the rhythm of it and the flow of it and try to get into what Bruce Barton was thinking when he wrote this line and then this line and where was he going. And you'll start to understand the letter. You can do this with all great letters, and you can become a much more powerful copywriter by doing this one single exercise.

It may seem like it's a little tedious unless you really get into the enjoyment of becoming a master copywriter by writing out famous letters in longhand, beginning with this one.

Craig: That's absolutely a proven technique. So even if it feels tedious, just know that it's a lot faster than doing all the years of self-discovery that Bruce Barton had to do to get it.

Joe: This is a shortcut. Well, he goes on then, and I love this because he says, "I have agreed to take ten boys and pay the deficit on their education each year, $1,000. I have agreed to do this if I can get 24 other men who will each take ten." There's a couple of things going on in here that I love. First of all, from a hypnotic stand-point, we have the phrase "I have agreed" twice. There's a little bit of a rhythm there, and you may find it hard to believe, but that's going into your brain and you're starting to agree. And you're hearing it twice.

In hypnosis, we usually repeat things very often. If you see a stage hypnosis, they don't say "You are getting sleepy" one time. They say, "You are getting sleepy, you are getting sleepy, you are getting sleepy." They are repeating the command so it goes into the brain. Here we have Bruce Barton saying, "I have agreed to take ten boys. . . . I have agreed to do this if I can get 24 other men who will each take ten."

The other thing that is going on, just in these two sentences, is that he seems to say, "Look, if I can do this, you can do this." He's not quite saying that, but he is saying, "I'm taking ten boys." So in the back of your mind, you are starting to think, "Is he going to ask me to take ten boys? Because I don't know if I can take ten boys. I don't know if he's going to say that. Surely he isn't going to ask us to take ten, so when he does get to what he's going to ask us to do, it's going to seem like a very small request compared to what we are imagining he's going to ask us to do." I just love this. Then he goes on to say, "I have agreed to do this if . . ." If!

That causes me to have a role in the outcome and success of that entire college and those ten boys who are just waiting to be helped by Bruce Barton. This will happen only if he can get some other people to help, meaning me, one of the readers of this. So, I love that in two sentences; he is in my head. He is controlling some of my thought processes. He's starting to get me to say yes. He's starting me to role-play what it's going to be like for me to chip in some money for the contribution to this college. I just love that that's happening in two sentences.

Craig: There are some other things here that this actually ties back to. In the fifth paragraph, it says, "This letter is being mailed to 23 men besides yourself, 25 of us altogether." And if you look now at what he's doing here, he's saying, "I'm in. I've agreed."

Joe: Yes.

Craig: But he's already put you all in the same group. So, it's not like us versus them or me and you. It's us. We're in it and he is. Now again, he still hasn't asked the reader for anything. But he's already said that he's agreed. And there are a couple of other things that I just noticed. When he referenced that one of the boys put himself through college and became a major in the United States Army, okay, that's a recognized and respected authority. All right? There's a missionary— obviously, a selfless good person, right?

And then what we have here, which I missed initially, is where he was talking about the students: "They are of the same stuff as Lincoln and Daniel Boone and Henry Clay."

Joe: Oh, good quote. That's a good catch.

Craig: There is nothing yet in this letter that you could look at and say anything bad about.

Joe: Right.

Craig: Everything is just pristine, perfect, and good-hearted, and without sin almost, it seems.

Joe: Yes, yes.

Craig: And so what you have here is that now he's in. He's gotten this deal. Yes, as you said, everything comes down to this, because remember, we have bought in now to wanting these folks to succeed. We want the Horatio Alger type story of "Hey, let's let Daniel Boone do whatever he's going to do." And that's where the tension comes in and that's when he's really turning on the pressure.

Joe: Those are great observations. I'm glad that you've elaborated on them and pointed them out. I had actually forgotten and quickly overlooked that one line, "They are of the same stuff as Lincoln and Daniel Boone and Henry Clay." That again awakens the noble. These are all wonderful people. It would be pretty hard to find anything dark about any of them, and he's saying the students at the college are of the same material as Lincoln.

Craig: And he's already established that he's telling you how it is.

Joe: Yes.

Craig: "There is another side to a man"—you know, he's telling you how it is. So, he's saying, they are of the same stuff. You've already let him into your head to tell you how it is. So, he's telling you who they are now. He's telling you the whole deal.

Joe: I love when he gets to "This is my proposition to you. Let me pick out ten boys, who are as pure-blooded Americans as your own sons," (interesting statement there) "and just as deserving of a chance. Let me send you their names and tell you in confidence, for we don't want to hurt their pride," (I love that because again, he's showing that he's thinking of people; he's imagining what they would be thinking and he's imagining what you might be guessing here) "where they come from and what they hope to do with their lives. Let me report to you on their progress three times a year."

There are so many things going on here. Maybe the key word is *involvement*, because he's not just asking for my money and then I'll never hear from him again. He's saying, "I will report to you, and it's coming from Bruce Barton. It's not like the college will report to you or some secretary will report to you. I, Bruce Barton, well-known author, advertising agency founder, and so forth, am going to take care of this personally, and I will give you reports and not just once, on Christmas Day." He's saying, "Let me report to you on their progress three times a year. You write me, using the enclosed envelope," (well, of course, that's traditional direct response marketing—enclose an envelope for the reply) "that, if and when I get my other 23 men, you will send President Hutchins your check." I think it's a nice little point here that he's not asking for any money to be sent to him.

Craig: Yes.

Joe: It's very important that he pointed out that you will send the money to the college president, not to Bruce

Barton. "If you will do this I'll promise you the best time you have ever bought for a thousand dollars." Well, this is starting to sound like the deal of the century, if not of my entire life, if not of most of history. It's sounding like I can make a difference for only a thousand dollars in somebody's life who could end up being another Lincoln or the equivalent.

And I'm also in a small, unique crowd of people who are making a difference in the world because I'm one of only 25. So, the involvement level, the ego level, and so forth are beyond initial comprehension.

Craig: And it's accelerating—the pace here. So much is happening in this paragraph, we could probably spend another hour just talking about this paragraph.

Joe: Yes. I'm noticing that, because if anything, it jumps right into, "Most of the activities to which we give in our lives stop when we stop." Boy, is this hitting home here. We're starting to talk about "You know, you've been doing well in your life and you might have money and all of that, but you know, your clock has got to stop at some point. And you know it."

Craig: And he's referenced your children. He's talked about how the young mountain folk are just as deserving as your children, right?

Joe: The next line is, "But our families go on." Oh, boy! Our families. "Young life goes on and matures and gives birth to other lives. For a thousand dollars a year you can put ten boys or girls back into the mountains who will be a leavening influence in ten towns or counties, and their children will bear the imprint of your influence." Now, this is appealing to status, to immortality, to ego; the psychology that's working behind all of this is incredibly hypnotic. And then his next line is, "Honestly, can you think of any other investment that would keep your life working in the world so long a time after you are gone?"

And at this point, I can't. Maybe I could have before I read this letter, but by the time I've gotten to this, it's like no. You know what, Bruce, I can't think of anything else that's going to be better than this. And this sounds like—a thousand bucks? Is that all you want?

Craig: Well, and he's even put that right on the table. "If you will do this I'll promise you the best time you have ever bought for a thousand dollars." He knows these people have the money. The question now is whether they are going to give it to Dr. William J. Hutchins, who, by the way, went to Yale.

Joe: That happens to have been mentioned in parentheses in the letter, by no accident.

Craig: So again, he is identifying that this money isn't going to go to some faceless charity or even some college. It's going to a specific person who will be shepherding their money, and Bruce Barton is going to be the ringleader here, and he's going to take the lead of the 25 people involved, right? He's going to do the dirty work. He's going to report and do all that stuff that realistically they probably don't want to do. But he's going to tell them how this story turns out, how their charges all succeeded.

He's going to keep the game going essentially, and it's a very honorable, deserving game. So, everyone involved—Henry Clay, Daniel Boone, your kids, and the Berea students—is of same stuff. We're all of the same stuff here. We're all heroes, and you just happen to have more money than these deserving people. But the one thing I really wanted to point out here is that you can see that folks will spend money on a movie ticket. They'll buy $20 popcorn or whatever it is, right, because of the experience.

This is something you remember Dan Kennedy writing about in his newsletter. You're going to get an experience for this thousand dollars, and what else are you getting? You're writing a check for what? These other folks are going to be going to the college, right? Your kids aren't even going to go there. But it's the experience and all these other feelings that he just machine-gunned—bam, bam, bam—and by the way, "after you are gone." That's a horrible phrase for the ego to think about—"I'm gone. I'm suffocating here. I'm going to get going. What do I do?"

Well, you, your family, and everybody who's all tied up together are going to be living on and be prosperous and be making the world better, and you are going to feel awesome about yourself when you are doing it.

Joe: I'm glad you pointed that out, because it reminds me: I had put out a little e-book one time called *Unspoken Marketing Secrets,* and I had a lot of ideas that were fairly controversial. But one of them I said in there was that people will spend any amount of money to have their psychological state changed. And it was coming from the perception that the old Thoreau thing, that the average person is living a life of quiet desperation. And most of us are dissatisfied with our lives. Well, Bruce began this letter by pointing out that "Yeah, I know you are dissatisfied with your life. I know that you are successful, but I know that it's incomplete because I know

I feel that way." So, he's established all of that. Now he's getting to the point where he's basically saying if you spend a thousand dollars, that internal feeling of dissatisfaction, that internal psychological state, will change.

Craig: And he's done all that here; absolutely, that is fantastic. And what you see is that he's actually not talking about anything different than the first two paragraphs. It's the same stuff. It's not long copy. He's not wandering all over the place. This is very precise. It may be indirect but it's precise. He's talking about that hole in your life of "What good are you anyway?" And he established what it is. He established the value of one particular place where your dollar will go further than anywhere else, and he just told you where to send a thousand of them.

Joe: Yes! I love it.

Craig: This is the solution to the hole he gave you at the beginning.

Joe: Yes. He created it and then gave you the solution for it. I love it. Well, he goes on in the ending paragraph, and I want to make sure we hit these two things because they are so important. "This is a long letter," he writes, "and I could be writing a piece for the magazines and collecting for it in the time it has taken me to turn it out." Well, Bruce Barton was very famous. He was a best-selling author. He wrote about 11 books. He was writing articles for major publications all the time.

He was the business celebrity of that decade. So, everybody would nod their head and say, "Yeah." He could have written an article and been on the front covers of whatever the magazines would have been at the time, and he would have been paid well for it. He did not have to do this. So, this is a reminder that "Look, I have taken the time to do this"—not actually saying that "It's really important I've done this," but he's implying that. "So, remember that this is different from any other appeal that ever came to you." Well, there's a sense of agreement because they are all thinking, "Yeah, I've never gotten a letter like this before. I've never heard this story before. I've never gotten something from Bruce Barton before."

He continues, "Most appeals are made by people who profit from a favorable response, but this appeal is hurting me a lot more than it can possibly hurt you," meaning that he's already agreed that he's going to be writing all of these people that give the money three times a year to give them reports; he's not making a dime.

In fact, he's going to do more than they are to keep that college going. So, he's really laying down the foundation again that "If I can do this, you can do this. And it's costing me a lot more than you. All you have to do is write a check once and then open some envelopes that will tell you the stories down the road." And then that last line, Craig, I love this last line. This is the ultimate in a close. This is so hypnotic. "What will you have, ten boys or ten girls?" There is no room for "no."

Craig: That's right.

Joe: There is no room for "Oh, you know, I don't want anything." No, it's like "Do you want ten boys or do you want ten girls?" This question is the most beautiful close that I can think of. Every time I read it, I say, "Ah, that is so brilliant!" I just love it. And it's only nine words, but in those nine words, he has established that you're doing this one way or another. So do you want ten boys or ten girls, and he wraps it up.

Craig: And he can wrap it up that succinctly, I believe, because a couple of paragraphs back he said, "You write me, using the enclosed envelope, that, if and when I get . . ." You know, he's telling them to get the envelope out; get your checkbook out. He's told them what to do. He's already done that. He's, again, commanding them what to do, even send it to President Hutchins. Send it for how much. There was nothing missing in the instructions. He's already told them how to relieve the pressure he has created.

Here he says, "This is a long letter," implying essentially, "You are still hanging with me here," so we're acknowledging a fact that you've just waded through a lot of paragraphs. But then he immediately says, "I could be writing . . ."; he could have been doing something else, too. So, you know your time is valuable. His time is valuable, and he's almost implying that his time is pretty darn valuable, thank you very much. Right? And then he doesn't ask this question, he tells them, "So, remember that this is different from any other appeal that ever came to you."

He doesn't ask them, "So don't you think, don't you agree?" No, he tells them how it is. When you get to the final line, he's been telling them how it is. "What will you have, ten boys or ten girls?" And if you bought in so far, you've got nowhere else to go.

Joe: Yes.

Craig: And there's no asking here in terms of—like you said, there's no "yes" or "no." It's "which," the assumed close.

Joe: Yes.

Craig: The psychological pressure and the greased chute, as it were, to the end of what he wants are so pristine. There is not an extra word in this letter, I don't believe. And that's worth the copying over that Joe was recommending earlier, if only for itself. There are no big, meandering words in here. There is no fluffy prose. Everything, every paragraph, has a purpose. Every paragraph has laid the foundation to get to this last sentence.

Joe: Those are great insights. The letter is written very simply and very directly. Even though he's writing to very educated people, very successful people, you don't find big words that you stumble over. He is writing as simply as if he was writing to a sixth-grade class somewhere and telling them stories. He's telling them stories just like he would tell to a bunch of schoolchildren.

Craig: But they are stories, as you pointed out; they are so loaded. You are un-American if you don't do this; Daniel Boone; Lincoln; Yale. It's all in there. You are one of the 25 superheroes who are going to save this town. If you don't do it, what are you?

Joe: Yes.

Craig: If you don't take the ten boys or ten girls, how are you going to feel, really? You know, another thing that just hit me is that if you are one of 25, he knows who you are.

Joe: That's a good observation.

Craig: Right. This isn't 25,000 people. It's "Oh, Mr. Smith from Jonesville. You are one of 25 and I know who you are."

Joe: Yes, that's a great observation. We can go on and on with this letter, so I'm going to end this by saying that the best advice I can add, besides just studying it and rereading this discussion because there have been a lot of insights by Craig and myself, is to write this letter out in longhand yourself and note what you find out on your own. In fact, you probably should write and tell me so I can share it with others down the road. But study this letter.

As a reminder, this letter went out in 1925. It got a 100 percent response. That meant every single person who got this did write back, sent in money, and chose ten boys or ten girls. And this is phenomenal. That is a miraculous, record-breaking event. So, study this letter. And Craig Perrine, of maverickmarketer.com, thank you very much for making this a deeper, wiser event. And Pat O'Bryan of patobryan.com, thank you for recording it for us. Thanks for listening. Joe Vitale, over and out.

BONUS:
THE WORLD'S FIRST
SPIRITUAL MARKETER

"Competition is no enemy, it is an ally, and when translated into service, it is a constant spur to betterment through more service and thus benefits all."
— J. C. Penney, *View from the Ninth Decade*, 1961

LET'S FACE REALITY

Y ou think you have it rough today?

Yes, there's war, poverty, depression, recession, economic uncertainty, competition, unfair business practices, and more.

I'm sure if you read today's newspaper and/or watched today's news, you could get depressed thinking about the current situation.

I'm sure if you went online and researched all the people selling a product or service similar to your own, you could also get yourself into a funk.

But let me ask you a question:

Is it really that bad?

Play along with me here. . . .

Imagine it's 1902.

You're living in a small town in Wyoming. Yes, Wyoming. Not exactly Chicago or New York City. Its population is only 3,000 people. They are mostly miners. They don't make much cash. And you can imagine what they do with it on payday.

There are 22 saloons in your city willing to take the miner's hard-earned money—and extend credit.

But let's paint the full picture here:

You don't have a phone, fax, computer, radio, television, or the Internet.

You don't have any money for newspaper advertising.

You're pretty poor yourself, with a wife and child to feed.

Your goal is to open a store selling clothing—at a discount.

And no one believes you can pull it off.

Every business owner and banker as well as most of your family and friends say you're nuts.

What are your chances for success?

Would you even attempt this enterprise?

Consider—and be honest with yourself:

Would you try to do business in that 1902 environment?

The truth is, I'm not even sure I would, and I'm a pretty positive-thinking kind of guy.

But a man with a vision can't be stopped.

(Remember that.)

A young man with a vision who in fact did start a small store in Wyoming in 1902, under all the conditions just spelled out, went on to create an empire that's still around today.

I'm talking about J. C. Penney.

Yes, the man who founded the famous department stores you can find in every major city (over 1,000 of them today) and where you probably bought your pants.

J. C. Penney rose from nothing to create a chain of stores originally called The Golden Rule. He made a fortune, and lost all of it—$40 million—in the Great Depression. But he also went on to become successful again, though never controlling the renamed company he began.

He loved people, was deeply religious, and made the people who ran his stores partners, not employees. He was a friend of Bruce Barton.

Clearly, Penney was a man quite different from others who walked the earth during his lifetime.

The store Penney opened in Kemmerer, Wyoming, on April 14, 1902, was in a one-room frame building located between a laundry and a boarding house off the main business district of the town.

He and his family lived in the attic over the store. The store was furnished with shelves made from packing crates.

Before opening, Penney studied the town, its people, and their needs. (Research always pays off.)

His store was called The Golden Rule because it emphasized the very principle he lived by. Virtually everyone in business said he would fail, especially when on moral grounds he opposed selling merchandise on credit. Yet the sales for the first day totaled $466.59 and for the first year they totaled $28,898.11.

Obviously, people liked the honesty of the 27-year-old visionary.

And what a vision he had.

THE VISION

Penney envisioned a chain of stores that would extend over the Rockies. To him, The Golden Rule represented more than a marketing strategy. It represented his deeper spiritual beliefs. It became the credo of his business. He insisted on offering customers quality merchandise at the lowest possible prices.

What a concept!

The strategy and the vision worked.

People loved it.

> "Exchange ideas frequently. If you and I exchange dollars we are no better off—each of us still has a dollar. If we exchange ideas we each have two ideas where we had one before. What you gave you have. What I got you did not lose. Share your ideas—you will not become poorer—both of you will be the richer for the mutual exchange."
>
> —J. C. Penney, speech on salesmanship, 1934

At the end of 1912, there were 34 Golden Rule stores with sales exceeding $2 million. (Imagine the wealth that represents even today.)

In 1913, the chain incorporated under the laws of the state of Utah as the J. C. Penney Company, Inc. Penney himself was opposed to the new name, but his partners outvoted him.

Still, Penney—the company and the man—maintained a spiritual vision to serve people.

In 1913, his company mission statement was:

To serve the public as nearly as we can to its complete satisfaction.

a. To expect for the service we render a fair remuneration and not all the profit the traffic will bear.

b. To do all in our power to pack the customer's dollar full of value, quality, and satisfaction.

c. To continue to train ourselves and our associates so that the service we give will be more and more intelligently performed.

d. To improve constantly the human factor in our business.

e. To reward men and women in our organization through participation in what the business produces.

f. To test our every policy, method, and act in this wise: Does it square with what is right and just?

As you can see, even his mission statement was unique.

(Thought: Can you adapt it for your own business?)

J. C. Penney is worth study and modeling today. That's why I've written this special report, which may be the first written work on him from a business viewpoint.

I've found that Penney, like Bruce Barton, cared about people to a degree rarely seen in any business.

For example, when his company was considering whether to accept credit cards, Penney objected, saying it would ultimately hurt the people, as it would encourage overspending. He was right, but the old gentleman cast the sole nay vote in a company he no longer controlled. He was overruled.

Still, you can sense his concern. While most people would be focused on all the ways to get money from their customers, Penney didn't want to make a profit at the expense of his customers' well-being.

This is rare.

(Ask yourself: Are you trying to drain your customers of their every dime, or are you trying to serve them while making a little profit for doing so?)

Penney was a deeply religious man, raised by a Baptist preacher who taught him self-reliance at an early age. When he was only eight years old, he was told he had to earn his own money for anything he wanted. Talk about self-reliance!

Penney later recalled in his autobiographical book, *View from the Ninth Decade*, that his father's announcement "came as an awful shock. . . . I went to bed feeling utterly cast off, and by my own father!"

But this strict upbringing and early training in self-reliance made him sensitive to the needs of others. It seems it was more than religious for Penney; it was also spiritual.

This very outlook helped Penney help others, too, as you'll see in this next section.

> "I believed then, as I believe today and shall to the end of my days, that when a man truly works with a principle, such as the golden rule, that principle makes him the representative of a great and positive working force. Then a creative force of the universe is back of him, for the principle is doing the work, while he merely attends to the details."
>
> —J. C. Penney, *Fifty Years with the Golden Rule*, 1950

SHARING WEALTH

I've often said that wealth gives you the means to help others, too. This is a very spiritual experience. Penney lived it, as well. For example:

In 1923, Penney established a 120,000-acre experimental farming community in northern Florida named Penney Farms. Some 20,000 acres were subdivided into small plots where industrious, moral, but economically destitute farmers could live and work until they could rebuild their lives.

Next to Penney Farms, he established the Memorial Home Community—a 60-acre residential community for retired ministers, lay church workers, missionaries, and their spouses and families—at a personal cost of more than $1 million.

Penney lost virtually all of his fortune in the stock market crash of 1929 and the subsequent Great Depression. While this certainly was a severe blow emotionally and financially, it did not stop him.

In 1954, after he had rebuilt his fortune, Penney established a second charitable foundation—the James C. Penney Foundation—which remains active today. This family foundation supports organizations addressing issues of community renewal, the environment, and world peace.

Obviously, Penney the man knew how to use his mind and his spirit to create wealth, and to use that wealth to help others.

He once said:

"Give me a stock clerk with a goal and I'll give you a man who will make history. Give me a man with no goals and I'll give you a stock clerk."

Obviously, J. C. Penney had a goal. It was to help the world. In his 95 years, he did his best. His name lives on today. He made history.

Penney was still coming to the office three days a week when he was 95.

(Note: Visionaries tend to regard work as a calling, not a vocation.)

He often expressed his desire to live to be 100 years old. But on December 26, 1970, he suffered a fall in his Park Avenue apartment that left him with a fractured hip. After weeks of recuperation, he died of a heart attack on February 12, 1971.

His middle name was Cash.

"Has business a soul? Has it any quality or characteristic by which it lives, thrives, and grows to majestic proportions? If there are things that disrupt and destroy business, there are also things that establish and perpetuate business. These elements are many—industry, frugality, fair dealing, self-respect, considerateness. But the soul of business is confidence."

—J. C. Penney, *Lines of a Layman*, 1956

YOUR CHALLENGE

I'll end this special report with a few challenges for you:

Do you have a goal?

As Penney pointed out, a goal can help you create history. Without one, you bounce around, tossed by the circumstances of life or the whims of your own unconscious mind.

As I explain in my book, *The Attractor Factor*, a goal creates a whirlwind of energy to help you go in the direction of whatever you want—including fame and fortune.

So, do you have a goal for your income?

Write your goal down here:

_____

_____

_____

_____

_____

Are you willing to do whatever it takes to achieve your goal?

People like J. C. Penney are willing to do whatever it takes to accomplish their goals. You may not have to do everything to reach the finish line, but you have to be *willing* to do whatever it takes.

Even after Penney lost his fortune in the Great Depression, he took time to recover emotionally, and then went forward to recover financially. He was willing to work.

Are you willing to do whatever it takes to create the wealth you seek?

Write your commitment here:

_____

_____

_____

_____

_____

Are you keeping your customers and clients in mind, thinking of more than money: thinking of how you can truly serve them?

Penney was able to create an empire—one you and I can see in every major U.S. city today—because he focused on the customer. He truly cared. He never wanted to profit at someone else's expense. His nobility is worth modeling today.

How are you giving people more than what they expect or even pay for?

Write down how you are serving people here:

_____

_____

_____

_____

_____

Where will you share your wealth?

As the life and work of J. C. Penney prove, people with a big goal, the desire to achieve it, and the focus on pleasing others can make a fortune—and leave a legacy. But these prosperous folks also know the value in giving their wealth away, too.

I contribute money, time, and service to many good causes. Here are a few:

- I've helped Paul Hartunian with his dog rescue mission at www.auntmarysdoghouse.com.
- Kevin Hogan and I have created a foundation to help children who have strokes shortly after birth at www.childrenneedingamiraclefoundation.com.
- I also started a foundation to help elevate the planet at www.IntentionalMeditationFoundation.com.

Contributing to these causes triggers a type of karmic marketing to kick in. As we help others, we are helped in return.

This concept is larger than what I can explain in this special report, but suffice it to say J. C. Penney and many other tycoons knew that you will receive your wealth in proportion to how much you give away. (And note that it's important that you give *now*, and not when you become wealthy. If you're not giving now, you won't give later. The idea is to activate this principle today.)

Are you willing to give money as you receive it?

Write down how you will use your wealth to help others:

_____

_____

_____

_____

_____

RESOURCES

J. C. PENNEY

Books Written by Penney

- *My Experience with the Golden Rule* (Kansas City, MO: Frank Glen Pub. Co., 1949).
- *Fifty Years with the Golden Rule: A Spiritual Autobiography* (New York: Harper & Brothers, 1950).
- *Lines of a Layman* (Grand Rapids, MI: William B. Eerdmans Pub. Co., 1956).
- *View from the Ninth Decade* (New York: Thomas Nelson & Sons, 1961).

Books about Penney

- *J. C. Penney: The Man with a Thousand Partners*, by Robert W. Bruere (New York: Harper & Brothers, 1931).
- *Main Street Merchant*, by Norman Beasley (New York: McGraw-Hill, 1948).
- *Creating an American Institution: The Merchandising Genius of J. C. Penney*, by Mary Elizabeth Curry (New York & London: Garland Publishing, 1993).
- *The Spiritual Journey of J. C. Penney*, by Orlando L. Tibbetts (Danbury, CT: Rutledge Books, 1999).

JC Penney Company Publications about Penney

- "James Cash Penney: His Life and Legacy." An 8-page mini-biography.
- "A Short History of JC Penney." A 4-page brochure outlining the history of the company over the past 100-plus years.

Further research can be done at:

The JC Penney Historical Archives
P.O. Box 10001
Dallas, TX 75301-4315
E-mail: amcilett@jcpenney.com
Fax: 972-431-4944

Also see: www.jcpenney.net/company/history/history/archive34.htm.

BRUCE BARTON

The only book by Barton still in print is his classic best seller, *The Man Nobody Knows*. However, some versions are rewritten or heavily edited, so I suggest you look in used bookstores for a copy of the 1925 original (it's not hard to find). One recent edition claims to "revive the primary source in Barton's original language" (Chicago: Ivan R. Dee, 2000). Here is a complete list of Bruce Barton's books, many of which are nearly impossible to obtain except through interlibrary loan:

Better Days (1924)

The Book Nobody Knows (1926)

He Upset the World (1931)

It's a Good Old World (1920)

The Making of George Groton (1918)

The Man Nobody Knows (1925)

Masters of Advertising Copy (1925)

More Power to You (1917)

On the Up and Up (1929)

The Resurrection of a Soul (1912)

What Can a Man Believe? (1927)

The Young Man's Jesus (1914)

All of Barton's letters and articles (thousands of them) and other materials are on file at the State Historical Society of Wisconsin in Madison.

There are several excellent unpublished papers on Barton:

Bruce Barton and the Twentieth Century Menace of Unreality, by Edrene Stephens Montgomery. PhD dissertation, University of Arkansas, 1984. (Contains an excellent bibliography.)

And There Arose a New King Which Knew Not Joseph: A Biography of Bruce Barton, by Robert Bedner. Senior thesis, Princeton University, 1947.

The Messiah of Business: A Study of Bruce Barton, by John F. Cook. Master's thesis, University of Wisconsin, 1962.

Bruce Barton: Editor, Author, Executive, by Joseph Meacham. Master's thesis, University of Wisconsin, 1964. (Probably the best and most complete biography of Barton.)

The Big Sell: Attitude of Advertising Writers about Their Craft in the 1920s and 1930s, by S. R. Shapiro. PhD dissertation, University of Wisconsin, 1969. (Includes a section on Barton.)

BOB BLY

Write for a complete catalog of books, special reports, and tapes by this prolific advertising genius: Bob Bly, 174 Holland, New Milford, NJ 07646.

JOHN CAPLES

This legendary copywriter left some priceless books. His most recent may be the best: *How to Make Your Advertising Make Money* (Prentice-Hall, 1983). One of his earlier books, *Making Ads Pay* (Dover, 1957), contains a couple of charming stories about Bruce Barton's ads.

DOTTIE WALTERS

To get a copy of Dottie's excellent book, *Speak and Grow Rich*, write: Walters Speakers Services, P.O. Box 398, Glendora, CA 91740.

THE SECRETS OF THE SECOND B IN BBDO: THE COPYWRITER NOBODY KNOWS

Dear Soon-to-Be Master Wordsmith:

I have put together an exclusive look into the mind of one of the greatest advertising geniuses in history.

His name is Bruce Barton. Ironically, as the author of *The Man Nobody Knows* and *The Book Nobody Knows*, he is now the Copywriter Nobody Knows. He was the second B in the famous BBDO ad agency.

Included is Bruce Barton's famous 1925 solicitation letter for Berea College. He sent it to 24 people. The result was a 100 percent return of about $30,000. It's considered one of the most effective letters ever written. See if you can detect why Barton's sales letter stratagems are so hypnotic.

You'll also be one of the very few people to be able to feast their eyes on actual Bruce Barton ads that were *not* shown during World War I for political reasons.

Much of the material presented here was culled from my personal research and the gracious contributions of my mentor, Joe "Mr. Fire" Vitale, who is the world's first hypnotic marketer and a Bruce Barton expert. Joe has distilled the stratagems of P. T. Barnum, John Caples, Robert Collier, and other legendary masters of ad copywriting into one system.

His system answers the question: "What will *you* do when you learn to hypnotize people with the power of words alone and get them to obey your commands?"

Keep the secrets found in this tour of Bruce Barton's mind to yourself, and use them wisely. They are very powerful indeed.

To your success,

Jo Han Mok

Jo Han Mok, The Master Wordsmith

The Story of the Second B in the BBDO (Batten, Barton, Durstine, & Osborn) Agency

There is a popular story that has gone around, saying that BBDO originated in an elevator in a Madison Avenue building. Apparently, Roy Durstine was riding up with William Johns, president of the Batten Company, and Johns remarked to Durstine, "Did it ever occur to you that we do *not* have any competing accounts?"

I think it is just a story and probably did not happen. It is a great one, though.

Alex Osborn, William "Papa" Johns, Bruce Barton (*BBDO Newsletter*, 1966, p.5).

Company executives meeting at Barton's desk (*BBDO Newsletter,* 1966).

However, in September 1928 the agencies did become one, and the chairman of the board was none other than Bruce Barton. The merged agency boasted 113 clients, 600 employees, and billings of $32.6 million in the first year—the year of the Great Crash (*BBDO Newsletter,* 1966).

> "Much brass has been sounded and many cymbals tinkled in the name of advertising; but the advertisements which persuade people to act are written by men who have an abiding respect for the intelligence of their readers, and a deep sincerity regarding the merits of the goods they have to sell."
>
> —Bruce Barton, summation of his advertising philosophy
> (*The Man Nobody Knows,* 1925, p. 153)

Barton was regarded as a religious quack by most. In his 1925 book, *The Man Nobody Knows*, he portrayed Jesus as the greatest advertiser who ever walked the face of this planet: persuading, recruiting followers, nailing all the right words that evoked emotional response and stirred desires.

Jesus epitomized modern salesmanship!

Barton had a really hard time getting it published because of the radical and controversial ideas it presented.

(Actually, Barton had even more controversial stuff on how the free enterprise system would create a heaven on earth.)

As a copywriter, one can see why Barton would see Jesus in this light.

Barton saw Jesus' parables as advertisements. In Jesus' metaphorical descriptions were embedded the principles he advocated to his disciples.

Barton felt that part of the reason Jesus was so successful in his undertakings was because of his genuine love for the people. Barton felt that great advertising had to be congruent. People were not as stupid as advertisers believed they were, and one of the reasons Barton stood out from his competitors was because he was always sincere—unlike his competitors, who were only interested in making the sales and fleecing people of their hard-earned money:

"It's time we quit trying to shear those sheep and start loving them!"

He wrote in his diary:

"I can, of course, continue to make people think that two gallons of gasoline just alike are not alike. But somehow it seems to me that the old day of competition is drawing to a close—that I should be laboring in the twilight of a passing era."

My personal favorite is this one:

"It is said that great leaders are born, not made. The saying is true to this degree, that no man can persuade people to do what he wants them to do, unless he genuinely likes people, and believes that what he wants them to do is to their own advantage."

THE SIX IMMUTABLE
LAWS OF ADVERTISING

A SHORT, SHORT COURSE IN COPY

Bruce Barton

In 1935 Bruce Barton laid down six copywriting rules in stone for the BBDO Operations Council, which they adhered to like the Laws of Moses. I personally regard the six rules as the greatest lesson in advertising *ever*.

1. *The theme:* Should be based on two principles—people are interested in themselves and they are interested in other people.
2. *Interesting headlines:* "Nobody was more surprised than I," said Barton, "when *The Man Nobody Knows* became a best seller. The title is what sold the book."
3. *The visualization.*
4. *The copy:* Eliminate the introduction. Copy should fit the space. "I never write a piece of copy without counting the words," Barton said.
5. *Adjectives:* When you finish, "go back and cut out all the adjectives."

6. *A purpose:* "Never write an ad without the idea that something is going to happen. What do we want the reader to do? . . . Remember the power of a direct command. Don't say, 'If you would like this beautiful booklet, we will be glad to send it.' Say, 'Sit down right now and fill in this coupon.'"

(BBDO Newsletter, 1966, pp. 42–43)

"In good times people want to advertise; in bad times, they have to."

—Bruce Barton, 1923

Here are the same six points, as decoded by Joe "Mr. Fire" Vitale:

LOST GENIUS REVEALS HOW TO WRITE SALES MATERIALS THAT SELL: OR, BRUCE BARTON'S SIX POINTS FOR WRITING ADS

Joe "Mr. Fire" Vitale

Bruce Barton was a celebrity in the 1920s. He was a best-selling author, confidant to presidents, master copywriter, philanthropist, congressman, and co-founder of the largest advertising agency in the world, BBDO.

He helped five men become U.S. presidents. He wrote a fund-raising letter that got a 100 percent response. The only book ever written on Barton and his ideas is *The Seven Lost Secrets of Success.* I recently discovered Barton's six points for writing ads, which he probably delivered in a speech in the early 1930s. Here they are, as Bruce Barton himself delivered them:

The Theme

"A lot of time and money is wasted by our failure to think through and get a theme before we start. The theme ought to be based on two principles—first, that a man is interested in himself; second, that he is interested in other people. Our formula for *Every Week* (magazine) was Youth, Love, Success, Money, and Health—all things in which people are vitally interested."

Interesting Headlines

"I think any public notice I may have had has come from titles. Nobody was more surprised than I when *The Man Nobody Knows* became a best seller. The title is what sold the book."

Barton also mentioned that when he edited magazines, he often used provocative titles for articles to stir up controversy and interest. Examples included, "Why I Never Hire Any Woman under 30," "How My Wife Has Hindered Me in Business," and the other side of the question, "How My Wife Has Helped Me in Business." These interesting headlines guaranteed readership.

The Visualization

Barton didn't elaborate on this. But I'm sure he was referring to the layout of any sales piece.

He once said, "A picture is worth two pages of type, and a headline is worth almost all the rest of the ad put together." For Barton, the illustration, headline, and body copy made up the layout, or visualization, of any sales piece.

The Copy

"The introduction can be eliminated almost always. The mind starts cold when you begin to write, and you don't get into high until the second or third paragraph. Cut out the introduction, and then you have a good hot start.

"Another elementary fundamental of advertising is to make the copy fit the space. To this day, I never write a piece of copy without counting the words. The picture, the headline, and the layout should be set before you begin the copy. To me, writing the copy before you have visualized the layout is backwards."

Adjectives

"After you finish a piece of copy, go back and cut out all the adjectives. Henry Ward Beecher's father was once chairman of a committee to draw up resolutions on slavery. One sentence in his resolution read: 'It is an outrage.' Someone suggested that it should read: 'It is a terrible outrage.' Beecher said that was the way he had it in his first draft, but he had cut out the word 'terrible' for the sake of emphasis. Adjectives are like the leaves on a switch. They make the switch look pretty, but if you want to hit a blow that will cut, you take off the leaves. Literature that cuts has very few adjectives. The greatest things in life are expressed in one-syllable words—love, hate, fear, home, wife, child."

A Purpose

"We should never write an ad without the idea that something is going to happen. What do we want the reader to do? Write with the conviction that he is going to do something when he gets through reading—go to the store and buy; clip the coupon and mail it. And remember the power of the direct command. Don't say, 'If you would like this beautiful booklet, we will be glad to send it.' Say, 'Sit down right now and fill in this coupon.'

Later in his life, Barton entered politics, and about one year before his death in 1967, Barton made a most memorable quote which summed up his life, "I am in the advertising business," (*BBDO Newsletter,* 1996, p.58).

People want things made easy; they want you to make up their minds for them."

One of the most important lessons Barton felt we could learn from Jesus is found on pages 157 and 158 of *The Man Nobody Knows*:

"Let him [the modern ad man] learn their [the advertisements'] lesson, that if you would teach people you first must capture their interest with *news*; that your service rather than your sermons must be your claim upon their attention; that what you say must be simple, and brief, and above all sincere—the unmistakable voice of true regard and affection."

THE ADS THAT
NOBODY KNOWS

These are rare, original ads by Barton. As you review them, see if you can spot his seven lost secrets at work.

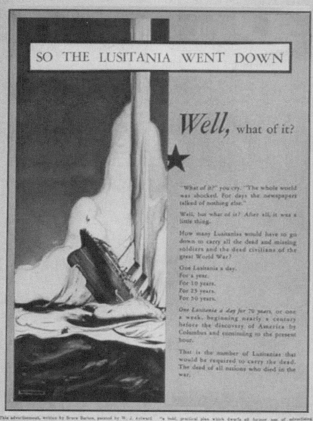

"Ideas are about the cheapest of all commodities. . . . But the supply of men who can execute ideas and make money out of them is pitifully small."

—Bruce Barton, 1936

Recommended Reading

Allen, Frederick Lewis. *Only Yesterday: An Informal History of the 1920s* (New York: Perennial Library/ Harper & Row, 1964). An entertaining and educational 1931 work. Brilliant.

Baida, Peter. *Poor Richard's Legacy* (New York: William Morrow & Company, 1990). Very readable introduction to the history of business values. Includes material on Barton.

Conwell, Russell H., Shackleton, Robert, and Collier, Robert. *Acres of Diamonds*. Wilder Publications, 1997.

Fox, Stephen. *The Mirror Makers: A History of American Advertising and Its Creators* (New York: William Morrow & Company, 1984; pap. ed., New York: Vintage, 1985). Fascinating in-depth look at advertising—including Barton's contribution.

Hattwick, Melvin. *How to Use Psychology for Better Advertising* (Englewood Cliffs, NJ: Prentice-Hall, 1950). A gem, long out of print.

Hopkins, Claude. *Scientific Advertising* and *My Life in Advertising* (New York: NTC Business Books, 1990). One of advertising's founding fathers tells his secrets in two classics from the 1920s. Worth memorizing.

Powell, Harford, Jr. *The Virgin Queene* (Boston: Little, Brown, 1928). Novel with the main character,

"Barnham Dunn," probably based on Bruce Barton. (The author had worked for Barton.)

Sackheim, Maxwell. *My First Sixty-Five Years in Advertising* (Blue Ridge Summit, PA: TAB Books, 1975). Out of print but worth hunting down. Insightful.

Schofield, Perry, ed. *100 Top Copywriters and Their Favorite Ads* (New York: Printer's Ink, 1954). Barton's work is of course included.

Watkins, Julian, ed. *The 100 Greatest Advertisements* (New York: Dover, 1959). Barton's work is in this classic several times.

White, Gordon. *John Caples, Adman* (Mandan, ND: Crain Books, 1977). The only biography of direct-mail king Caples. Includes brief sections on Barton.

Bibliography

Applegate, E., ed. *The Ad Men and Women: A Biographical Dictionary of Advertising.* Westport, CT: Greenwood Press, 1994.

Barton, Bruce. *The Man Nobody Knows.* Indianapolis, IN: Bobbs-Merrill Company, 1925.

"The BBDO Century." 1991. *Advertising Age supplement,* 1991.

BBDO 1891—100 Year Anniversary Book. New York: BBDO, 1991. Internal publication.

BBDO Newsletter—75th Anniversary. New York: BBDO, 1966. Internal publication.

"Creative Quotations from Bruce Barton." 2001. www. bemorecreative.com.

Floyd, A. 1999. www.ciad.org/studies/student/99_fall/ theory/floyd/barton/index.html.

Fox, Stephen. *The Mirror Makers: A History of American Advertising and Its Creators.* New York: William Morrow & Company, 1984.

Lears, J. *Fables of Abundance: A Cultural History of Advertising in America.* New York: Basic Books, 1994.

Marchand, R. *Advertising the American Dream.* Berkeley, CA: University of California Press, 1985.

Index

About Dr. Joe Vitale

D r. Joe Vitale is president of Hypnotic Marketing, Inc. a star in the movie, *The Secret,* and
an author of far too many books to list here.

He is the author of the international best seller *The
Attractor Factor: 5 Easy Steps for Creating Wealth (or
Anything Else) from the Inside Out,* as well as *The Greatest
Money-Making Secret in History!, Hypnotic Writing,* and
the best-selling Nightingale-Conant audioprogram,
The Power of Outrageous Marketing, and numerous other
works.

He has written books for the American Marketing
Association and the American Management Association,
including *The AMA Complete Guide to Small Business
Advertising.* His most recent books are *Zero Limits,*
co-authored with Dr. Ihaleakala Hew Len, and *Buying
Trances.*

To browse an online catalog of his books and tapes,
to read dozens of free articles by him, or to sign up for
his free e-newsletter, see his main web site at www.
MrFire.com.